Rosa May:
The Search For A Mining Camp Legend

by George Williams, III

Tree By The River Publishing
P.O. Box 935
Dayton, Nevada 89403

Rosa May: The Search For A Mining Camp Legend
by George Williams III

Published by:
Tree By The River Publishing
P.O. Box 935-RM
Dayton, Nevada 89403

Other non-fiction books by George Williams III:

The Redlight Ladies of Virginia City, Nevada *(1984)*
The Guide to Bodie and Eastern Sierra Historic Sites *(1982)*
The Murders at Convict Lake *(1984)*
The Songwriter's Demo Manual and Success Guide *(1984)*
Mark Twain: His Life In Virginia City, Nevada *(1986)*
Mark Twain: His Adventures at Aurora and Mono Lake *(1987)*
Mark Twain: Jackass Hill and the Jumping Frog *(1988)*
Hot Springs of the Eastern Sierra *(1988)*
In The Last of the Wild West *(1991)*

Library of Congress Cataloging-in-Publication Data
Williams, George, III, 1949-
  Rosa May, the search for a mining camp legend.
  Bibliography: p.
1. May, Rosa, 1855-ca. 1912. 2. Prostitutes—Nevada—Biography.
3. Prostitutes—Nevada. 4. California—History—1850-1950. 5. Nevada—
History. 1. Title. HQ145.N3W54 1982   306.7'42'0924   82-11154
ISBN 0-935174-0709

Printed in the United States of America

Preface to Twelfth Printing

Rosa May: The Search For A Mining Camp Legend details a three year search I undertook to uncover the truth behind the legend of Rosa May, a mining camp prostitute who worked the brothels of Virginia City and Carson City, Nevada during the 1870's, 80's and 90's who eventually settled in Bodie, California, now a ghost town, where she is buried in the outcast cemetery.

This book is written for readers who have visited Bodie and for those who have not. Bodie visitors will learn about Rosa May and Bodie history. Those who have not been to Bodie will find the writing visual; Bodie, the land and the people are described.

Those interested in Carson City and Virginia City history will find information here concerning the brothels, madams and prostitutes of those towns.

Historians and Old West buffs may discover new research methods that might help with their individual projects.

Finally, to those Western Americana purists who may object to the inclusion of certain personal information: there were two ways I could have written this book. One, knock out another dull historical text or two, attempt to involve the reader by explaining how I became fascinated with the Rosa May legend, detailing step by step the methods I used to uncover her story. This second method was more dramatic. I felt the drama would help to hold reader interest while at the same time providing historical information about Rosa May and mining camp prostitution in the American West. There was a risk in doing this, but I believed the risk was worth it.

In recent years there has been much interest in the role of women in settling the American West, and to a larger degree, a new interest in women studies in general. It is my hope that this book will help people understand the difficulties the 19th century American woman faced.

It has been sixteen years since I first began researching the Rosa May legend, and twelve years since this book's first publication.

When I began my work I was young, ignorant and unsuccessful. But I had desire and I was stubborn. And in the end, what Ignorance could not discover, Tenacity revealed.

In looking over the book again, I feel a fond admiration for that young fool who scoured the Nevada and California desert in a beat-up Volkswagen looking for—hell, I really didn't know what I was looking for. I had a gut feeling it was something I should do and with some foolishness and passion went forward. I'm glad I did. I hope I will be so foolish and passionate with my future writing endeavors.

George Williams III
Carson City, Nevada
Spring, 1991

For my wife,
Edie Karen Williams,
without whose love, belief, and
encouragement, this book could
never have been written.
Thank you.

*Like as a father pitieth his children, so the Lord
    pitieth them that fear him.
For he knoweth our frame; he remembereth that
    we are dust.
As for man, his days are as grass; as a flower of the field,
    so he flourisheth.
For the wind passeth over it, and it is gone; and the place
    thereof shall know it no more.
But the mercy of the Lord is from everlasting to
    everlasting upon them that fear him, and
    his righteousness
    unto children's children...*

Psalm 103:13-17

Book I

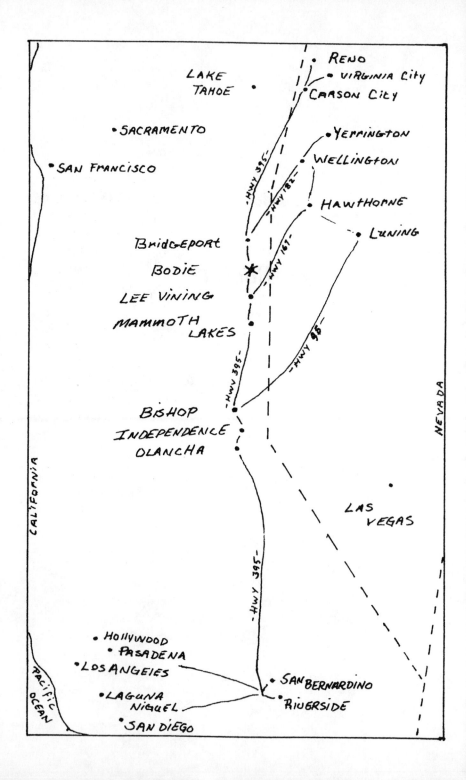

Chapter 1

If you ever come to the ghost town of Bodie, California, you will find her as I found her. She is buried in the outcast cemetery just beyond the barbed wire fence. Someone cut the last rung of wire in the fence near her grave and there is a hole there now. Each year, thousands of visitors crawl through the hole to reach her grave. Today, the dirt about her grave is beaten bare by many who want to know who this is, buried in the outcast cemetery.

Her peculiar gravestone stands far from others with none to keep it company. The base of the gravestone is a rectangular slab of concrete. Standing on this is cemented another concrete slab, several inches narrower in width and slightly curved at the top. The top portion of this slab was meant to be a smooth, evenly cut curve as with some of the finer stones in the cemetery above. But this craftsman, lacking patience or the proper tools, cut a jagged curve and the top portion is oddly lopsided. The standing slab is painted white and with its lopsided top resembles an ice cream cone that has slowly melted. Hard mountain weather has blasted the paint away in patches and the raw concrete shows through. It is surprising that any paint remains on her marker after all these years.

With her gravestone in such ragged condition it is certain remaining family members no longer live nearby. If so, they would have eagerly whitened her marker long ago.

The letters of her name were carved into the marker when the concrete was soft and pliable. The printed letters are contorted and child-like. Printed is her first name and, below, what sounds like her middle name. The marker appears to be without the woman's birth and death years. But if you stoop down and carefully examine the stone you will find "1880" faintly scribbled.

One takes 1880 as the year she died. Yet the date is so faintly scribbled, one wonders whether or not the stone maker was certain himself of the woman's time of death.

Above her name, a red cross is carved deep and wide into the concrete. The blood red cross of Christ burns brightly against the white marker like a blessing.

At the base of the gravestone where the two slabs are cemented together, there is an imprint of a tiny shoe. One feels that the shoe must have belonged to the woman buried beneath. Still, the shoe imprint seems strange.

Beside the shoe imprint are written two words: "by Serventi." The name is obviously Italian. Was this woman Italian? Was Serventi her husband, her brother or a lover? Or was Serventi simply the Bodie undertaker? Perhaps Serventi was a friend who made the poor woman this marker out of kindness. Though his tribute is lopsided and unprofessional, the marker's flaws make her seem more human, more worthy of pity.

Whoever Serventi was and whatever she was to him, he had cared enough for the woman to haul this three hundred pound stone up the hill to mark her otherwise anonymous grave.

Those who find her gravestone outside the fence believe that she is buried beneath it. They do not know that her gravestone was made years after her death and placed here by a man who never knew her nor exactly where she is buried. He unknowingly placed her gravestone one hundred and fifty feet from where she is actually buried.

Long ago, when she was buried, a square wood fence was placed around her grave. Those who supposedly loved her made the fence but did not bother to make a headstone with her name, birth and death years. Only the anonymous fence. Each side of the fence was square and two boards ran crisscross, making each side look like a square with an X inside.

That is how her outcast grave looked a very long time ago before someone tore the fence down. With the fence gone, there was nothing left to mark her grave. Sagebrush moved in and swallowed the mound of earth as if to hide her grave from any who might seek to find it.

It took a long time of searching before I found an early photograph of the Bodie cemetery that shows exactly where her grave is. The photo was taken in 1927 and shows the entire Bodie cemetery and various landmarks in the town beyond. Her crisscross fence stands far from other marked graves, by itself in the outcast cemetery.

I took that photo and had an 8x10 and a 5x8 copy made. Photos in hand, I searched the lower slopes of the outcast cemetery for her grave. I found many graves in a forest of sagebrush. It was difficult to determine which was hers.

Using landmarks in the 1927 photo of the Bodie cemetery I finally located her grave after several days of careful searching. The grave was so thickly overrun with sagebrush that I had to chop it down with an axe. After I cleared the sagebrush away, I piled stones on her tiny mound so that the grave would not be lost again. Locating her grave was somewhat of a victory for me. It had taken three obsessed years to learn her story and locate her actual grave. In that time of labored searching, we had become friends in a strange sort of way.

When she was very young, her dreams were beat out of her by a stern man and woman who lacked imagination and intelligence. They were unhappy that life had brought them so little. They had given up dreaming long ago. It was foolishness. Whenever they looked at their pretty and intelligent daughter and saw how her eyes glistened, how they hoped and dreamed; they became angry with her. They scolded and criticized her needlessly until the dullness in their eyes began to grow in hers. They made her believe that anything as worthless as herself could never have the dreams she dreamed. She became angry with her parents and inwardly angry at herself. Someday she would make them suffer the pain she had endured all those years while living with them.

The sternness and lack of imagination of her father and mother eventually broke her faith in herself and in her future. She was headed for a terrible tragedy. Still her soul longed for freedom— freedom from her parent's chastising and freedom from something she did not understand. Someday when she was old enough she would leave her parents, go far away and never come back.

She came West to Virignia City, Nevada in the mid-1870's when that mining camp was full of silver and freedom seekers like herself. She was just another pretty thing that ended up on "the line." For nearly twenty years she wasted her youth in Virginia City and Carson City whorehouses. One morning in 1892 she awoke to discover she was thirty-seven.

Thirty-seven. She was too old now for the high-class brothels. She was no longer the attractive young thing she once was. She had never looked far enough into the future to see herself growing old losing her beauty and her appeal. The rosy color of youth was gone from her cheeks. She needed more of the pink powder fluffed on her face to compete with the young girls who were taking her place and making the kind of money she once made. In the mirror she saw the lines that cracked about her mouth and the lines that spread from her eyes like sullen rays of doom. And yes, she had to admit, she had put on some weight. Her arms were fleshy, her thighs and butt were thicker, there was more weight in her face. Her being so stout made it all the more apparent. But there was something in her eyes now that had not been there years before. It was a cold steely hardness. It had come from too many years of too many men. It had come from too many years of hustling, too many years of scrounging from one whorehouse to the next, too long a time of reckless living. It had all caught up with her at last. Sure, part of "the life" had been fun, but the fun was gone out of it. Now the hardness was in her eyes and it would not go away. The customers saw it and it made them not want to go up the stairs with her. She knew men liked the young stuff. Why hadn't she seen this moment coming?

It didn't matter. The madams had. They had kept her on too long as it was. They had fed her, clothed her, and taken care of her when she was young and still had something to offer. Now her

4

youth was gone and her beauty was quickly fading. They put her out in the streets.

For years she had known the security of the madam telling her what was right and wrong. Now that substitute parent was gone. As she stood on the lonely street, the biting winter wind crawled up the sleeves of her coat. The sudden, shattering loneliness crept into her stomach. She couldn't shake it off. She couldn't believe after all these years it could come to this.

She looked through her past searching for someone to run to, someone to save her. She remembered Ernie, Ernest Marks. She had loved Marks a long time ago when they were young but he did her dirt like the rest, she always made them do her dirt. But at times he had been good to her. Marks ran a saloon in Bodie now, it was called the Laurel Palace. She knew Bodie wasn't the mining camp it used to be but that might be a good reason to go there.

The gold camp of Bodie had boomed in 1879 just as Virginia City began her long decline. The greedy opportunists knew Virginia City had few years of prosperity left and struck out for the new camp.

From 1879 until 1882 Bodie saw high times. Gold was plentiful and men and women were eager to get to Bodie. As with all mining camps, Bodie's boom collapsed when production of high grade ore declined. Of Bodie's population of ten thousand, eight thousand deserted Bodie pronto. They headed for the Colorado strikes and other new and promising camps.

About two thousand stayed on, mostly miners and their families. Bodie settled down to a regular small town of white frame cottages with mining its one and only industry.

During the 1890's, the camp would have died then and there if the cyanide process had not been discovered and introduced into the Bodie mining facilities. This new process of gold extraction gave Bodie a new lease on life. With the cyanide process the camp was able to support a population of about fifteen hundred. Most of these people stayed because they believed Bodie would one day boom again. Always after the fall, there remained those who believed the boom camp would rise again. Few ever did.

About 1892, at the age of thirty-seven, she came to Bodie. Bodie was no longer the boom camp it once was, and she; no longer the woman she had been. The dying mining camp of Bodie was ideal. There would be less competition here. The smart young whores would be drawn to the boom camps.

She moved into a little white house on Bonanza Street in Chinatown, the low part of town far to the north end. Here for twenty more years she introduced young Bodie males to sex. She comforted the lonely butcher whose wife thought sex too dirty or too inconvenient. She held her door open for the ugly misfits no woman would have and gave the middle aged man his last fling before the long decline. She took on chinks and blacks; whites and indians; farmer, lawyer, banker, miner, rancher, cowboy; high and low; big and small, anyone with a buck. And all the time she drank more because that dying light in her soul reminded her morning after sleepless morning that it had all been a waste. She had not made the world pay for her pain. She was growing old and she was not loved. The overwhelming sadness haunted her.

There were women in Bodie who hated her. Their stinging eyes followed her when she came uptown to browse in the shops. She had put up with the angry eyes of such women for so long that their staring no longer bothered her. And this only made the women who hated her more angry. But it gauled them to see their sons and daughters waiting in the streets for the woman from Chinatown. The children all knew how the dark haired woman from Chinatown handed out dimes as if the silver coins were birdseed. And a dime for any Bodie child was a great meal ticket to Cecil Burkham's candy counter.

Though she troubled some of Bodie's women, the Bodie men did not think twice about her. In their time, her kind was taken for granted. Such women were little gifts from God, fathers brought their virgin sons to, lonely men went for temporary comfort and middle aged men went to reaffirm their fading manhood. Certainly she wasn't the kind of girl you brought home to Mom. She was simply a fact of life and useful sometimes. So

6

the men did not run her out of town. In fact, the money they paid her provided her with a means of living and gave her a niche in their community. Though she was as much a part of their town as the blacksmith or the butcher, few men would have admitted this.

One November when the snow was deep and the grey sky shivered and the acid wind ripped across the barren hills, her few friends dragged her corpse out of town on a sled. She had not died a happy death.

The handful of Bodie women who hated her finally had their revenge. They put up a huge fuss and would not allow her friends to bury her among the decent folk in the higher cemetery. The men who lived in Bodie and had been her clients for over twenty years did not speak up to defend her. They did not want to hurt or embarass their families. Her friends were forced to bury her on the lower slopes of the cemetery outside the fence. As the cold wind tore across their faces and blew snow into their eyes it was not easy to break the frozen earth with their pickaxes.

She had always loved the mountains. She felt protected by the huge mounds of earth and stone surrounding her. The mountains were like fortresses safeguarding her from the outside world. And as if to please her, two of the most famous mining camps ever — Virginia City and Bodie — had sprung up at the foot of mountains surrounded by other mountains.

In Virginia City, she had lived many years beneath towering Sun Mountain. Each day as the sun slid behind the mountain and the mountain's shadow crept over Virginia City, she began her workday. Her workday ended with the first light creeping over the mountains east of town.

In Bodie, her tiny white cottage lay at the foot of Bodie Bluff, the barren, sage-ridden mountain, men climbed and dug the gold out of. Here, as in Virginia and Carson City, the town was emcompassed by the barren Bodie Hills and they had made her feel protected.

Bodie was by far the most rugged and isolated mining camp she had lived in. At 8,372 feet, winter came early and lasted a good eight months. With winter came the fierce cold and the snow that nearly covered the houses in snowdrifts cutting the camp off from the outside world. Only the heartiest efforts got a man in and out. Bridgeport, the nearest town, was twenty miles away and it took the man who carried the mail by horse and sled, one full day to make the trip from Bridgeport to Bodie.

To the north and down Bodie Canyon, there was Aurora, seventeen miles away. Aurora was another mining camp and as isolated as Bodie. There were train connections to Carson City at Hawthorne, Nevada, thirty-six miles away — but Hawthorne was even more difficult to reach than Bridgeport.

She had not minded the isolation. She had come to Bodie because of the isolation and it was the isolation that kept her there so long. As the years slipped by she had grown to need the isolation more and more. For with the years, truth had become more deadly. Truth, which had always chased her like a dog chasing his tail, had caught up with her with age despite Bodie's isolation.

The Bodie Hills have changed little in the millions of years since volcanoes erupted and spewed lava in all directions forming the Hills and leaving them covered with basalt forever. The deep brown and burned basalt is often canyon walls high or strewn about the Hills in huge chunks, in places making the land look more like a lunar surface than earth. The barren, basalt Hills are as lonesome and as wild as ever and for the majority of their existence man has had little to do with them. There were the Piutes who trotted through them during summer and collected pinon nuts in the fall. And there were the white men who roamed and mined in the Hills from the 1850's on after Aurora boomed. But for the most part, men have left the Hills alone. Men had little to do with them before gold was discovered and have little to do with them now that the gold is gone.

The Bodie Hills lie east of the Sierras, south of Bridgeport Valley and north of Mono Lake, a monstrous sea of brackish water fed by the runoff of the Sierras and surrounding hills. In the Bodie foothills, the sagebrush grows hip high and there is much rabbit brush, yellow flowered when blooming. The foothills are pea green colored from the sagebrush and the slivers of grass that grow in the sandy soil between the sage and basalt. Dark green, cone-shaped pinon pines dot the lower foothills. But as the Hills rise in elevation, there are fewer pinon pines and the sagebrush no longer grows hip high. In order to survive the severe cold and wind in the higher Hills, the sagebrush has cropped itself and grows in stouter bushes.

During summer, the higher Hills are green from the sage-brush. In a few canyons where water collects, stands of aspens, small and twisted by the snow and wind, struggle for survival. The pinon pines do not grow in the higher Hills and but for the few canyons of aspens, the Hills are barren of trees.

In the spring, the snow begins to melt and the black earth returns in patches. The wind blows the remaining snow into huge white strips and the Hills are zebra marked. Patches of snow will remain on the Hills through mid-summer where the snow has piled in drifts. Though summer days are warm enough for a man to go bare chested, nights will freeze standing water.

In the spring, the melted snow curls down the canyons in skinny creeks and drains into the flat places between hills and the grass is thick and moist in the flat places. There are springs too, in the mouths of canyons and the spring water is very good and cold. Small animals — rabbits, chipmunks, ground squirrels and deer drink at the springs and feed on the lush grass beside the water.

By mid-summer, the Hills are beautiful with wild flowers, the fields of blue and white lupin, the red Indian Paintbrush, the wild daisies, the irises and the fried-egg flowers — all white with a large yellow center.

In summer, the sky is wide and blue with huge islands of

cumulus clouds. The air smells very fresh and wild, mostly from the rich pungent smell of the white sagebrush. Depending on the summer, between every five days and two weeks, the cumulus clouds gather into black thunderheads and storm the Hills. The storms are brief, for an hour or so but the rain falls full and hard. Afterwards the Hills smell wonderful with the damp, wild smell of the wet sage. It is an unmistakably fresh fragrance you easily fall in love with and miss when you are away from.

By September, nights in the Bodie Hills have grown bitterly cold. By October the long hard winter has set in. In a short time the snow comes and the green, sage covered Hills become white until the June warmth returns.

In the narrow valley below her grave, what remains of the boom camp she knew stands for all who care to see it. The wood frame buildings are brown and cracked from so many hard winters. The years have stripped their paint coverings. They stand naked to the wind, cold and heat. Their elderly sides lean in, roofs are caving in, windows are cracked or missing. Outhouses have fallen and rot where they lay. Heaps of tin and broken glass are scattered through the dead settlement. Model T's rust in the fields. Wooden wagons stand unattended. Cattle gather in empty lots where houses and saloons once stood. They leave their droppings behind them without shame.

In the early morning, in the evenings or at intervals during the day when visitors have packed up and crawled back to the highway, it is then that you come to know Bodie best and learn why it is that places like this are called ghost towns. The streets are naked of concrete and tar, naked too of the people who lived beside them and walked them day after day. They are gone now, it is still and lonely. A slight wind comes up. The saloons are dusty and empty, the cottages are without miners and their families, their church is without worshipers, their school house empty of children's noises, their giggles, shouts and whimpers, all gone.

Bodie Bluff, a steep hill just east of town, is without the beehive of miners and wagons that once crawled over the mountain seeking its golden honey. The huge mound of dirt and rock is pitted and gouged where men dug for gold. The mountain looks ravaged as if some beast dug into its sides and tore from the depths something vital and necessary for survival. There are piles of rock and golden sand beside the beast's holes. From one hole to the next are paths, mere lines from a distance. The paths are no longer traveled nor are the holes and piles of rock bothered with any longer. The people who lived here have no use for Bodie Bluff now that its gold has been harvested. They have deserted the mountain and their houses. They are gone.

As you walk up deserted Main Street, you pass the Miner's Union Hall. For years it has missed the clomp of miner's boots. Farther down, there is Harvey Boone's general store with its elaborate door and window moldings. They speak of a more extravagant era. There is a barber's shop without customers, a stable without horses or blacksmith, a Chinese washhouse, an assay office.

But it is the Standard Mill that is most obvious. The mill is enclosed in grey corrugated steel. Several windows are broken out. Three rusting smoke stacks stick out of the roof like long fingers reaching for the sky. There is a rusted flag pole where the patriotic once raised their flag. Strewn about the Standard are assorted discarded mining machinery. A rusting engine, rusting iron pipe, the squashed body of and early car. Long ago the pounding of the Standard was heard day and night at any part of town. Its thunder filled the tiny valley and reached out for several miles. The people of Bodie did not mind the incessant pounding. The Standard was the heart of their community. They wondered and feared whenever its roaring ceased. The pounding only stopped when the machinery broke down or when the pipes froze in winter. Otherwise, the mill ran continually, pounding tons of gold-quartz into powder, assuring the people that the ore from Bodie Bluff would last forever.

At the end of north Main Street there are piles of waste rock from the mines. The gold and red rock is now the home of various little animals. A chipmunk scurries over the rocks. A ground squirrel stands poised until you come too near. Then he squeaks his warning cry and dashes for his home.

In empty lots, roaming cattle munch the moist grass. A heifer moos for her stray calf. The calf comes running to her. He plunges his head into her milk sack and sucks her brown nipples. Across town a lone bull calls to his herd. He haws and haws until they begin to follow him up one of the canyons. The bull's hawing echoes through the still valley. Blackbirds follow the cattle, the glistening black feathers of the male birds, the dull grey feathers of females, their click-click bird talk can be heard. Flies buzz in your ear and about the piles of fresh manure.

You walk into the sage covered lots behind Main Street. There are rows of tiny cottages here. The sagebrush grows thick and high beside them. It grows thicker every year as if it longs to topple the houses. The roofs of the cottages are covered with squares of tin cut from large containers and tacked to the roof to keep out rain and snow. A loose piece rattles in the wind.

Lots beside the houses are strewn with more rubbish, rusting tin, broken windows, heaps of green and violet glass, busted pipe, scattered chunks of brick, foundations of buildings that have long burned down, holes where outhouses once stood and large round holes where water was hauled out in buckets. The wells are filled now with rocks, timber and trash. They are useless.

As the summer sun dips toward the western hills, shadows begin to curl about the Bodie buildings and in the streets. The air becomes chilly. You watch the barn swallows as they flutter up to their mud nests beneath the roof of the assay office. You see the tiny baby birds open their yellow mouths as the parent birds steadily flutter, dunking food into the eager mouths.

You walk up Main Street and you imagine the world that once lived on this very street so long ago. The clomp and snorting of horses is gone. The shouting of boys off to baseball games is gone. The rattling wagons, the pounding of the stage, the giggles of adolescent girls, the heated talk of miners and speculators, the searing language of whores, gamblers and drunks, all gone.

Chapter 2

It's hard to believe that three years have passed since I first visited Bodie and stumbled onto Rosa May's grave in the outcast cemetery. I had no idea that July day that I would spend the next three years researching and chronicling the life of one of Bodie's legends. The last thing on my mind was setting about researching anything, not to mention writing a book. Only a year out of college where I had spent most of the last seven years, I for once, had my fill of books and research papers.

I was just another tourist that day, one of thousands who each year bump their way over the dirt roads for a glimpse of the old West. Like many before me, I discovered Rosa's legend told in books and by word of mouth by the area's residents: the story of a good hearted prostitute who died one winter long ago while nursing miners through a pneumonia epidemic. Despite Rosa's efforts to save lives, she was denied burial in the cemetery.

The injustice of Rosa's story angers many. For the unforgiving act of burying the kind hearted Rosa May outside the fence, seems a brutally cold thing to many today. Yet in Rosa's day, shortly after the turn of this century, such ostracism was common.

Rosa's story reminded me of the adulteress who was dragged before Jesus by an angry mob about to stone her. Badgering Jesus, the mob attempted to force him to decide what they should do with the woman; for according to the law of Moses, they were commanded to stone her to death. But Jesus turned from the mob as if he had not heard them and kneeling, began to write with his finger in the sand. One wonders whether Jesus wrote down each man's name and a few sins they had committed. And as they continued to badger Jesus, he stood and said: "He that is without sin among you, let him first cast a stone at her." Convicted by their own consciences, one by one, beginning with the eldest, the men walked away. Left alone with the woman, Jesus said to her: "Woman, where are your accusers? Has no man condemned you?" She answered: "No man, Lord." "Neither do I condemn you: go and sin no more."

It's a wonderful story. If each of us could be so forgiving.

Today the outcast grave of Rosa May reminds us that once, long ago, there was an unforgiving people, who, like Rosa, have since passed on.

I found many during my research who hold Rosa's story dear. Many identify with her injustice. The reason is simple: each of us has at some time been treated unfairly. We seldom forget such experiences or those responsible.

Rosa May's outcast grave represents to these people, the part of them that has at one time experienced injustice. They feel akin to Rosa because they have shared similar experiences. And because they feel a part of her, they are able to have compassion for her. Many of these people, like myself, are curious to know who Rosa May really was; why did she become a prostitute; where did she come from; what was her life really like; is there any truth to her legend? For the thousands who have come to Bodie and asked these questions there have never been any real answers until now.

In the three years since I discovered Rosa May's outcast grave, in my obsessed search for her story I have traveled twenty thousand miles by car with very little money; scoured every relevant city, county, state, national and church record; scrutinized hundreds of photographs; devoured sixty books and numerous articles, forty years of newspapers; wrote one hundred and sixty research letters; interviewed every one of Bodie's survivors; spent hundreds of hours in museums, libraries and courthouses, thousands of hours piecing her life together.

The work was worth the reward. Three years of tedious searching has uncovered some answers to Rosa's curious life. I believe I understand why she chose to prostitute herself.

This is the story of how I unearthed Rosa's life from gossip, myth and fact.

Chapter 3

Three summers ago, myself and a good friend, Kevin Lamb, were hired as entertainers at Mammoth Lakes, California, a popular ski and summer resort three hundred miles north of Los Angeles, high in the eastern Sierras. During our stay at Mammoth Lakes I visited nearby Bodie and became interested in the legend of Rosa May.

Surrounded by mountains and wilderness, Mammoth Lakes prospers year long. In the higher country above the resort are the series of green lakes from which Mammoth Lakes takes her name. The lakes are in steps, each slightly higher in elevation than the next. When spring comes, the warm weather drives the melted snow down from the high peaks through steep canyons into the lakes. The water flows freely from the higher lakes to the lower lakes and finally down a rocky canyon through the forest and the resort. Mammoth Creek, as it is then called, provides fine trout fishing when the water warms. The Creek waters the valley, feeding the moist green plants and wild flowers that thrive beside its sweet waters.

During the 1870's and 80's, men searched Mammoth Creek and the mountains for gold. They found gold in what is known today as Old Mammoth. Here, for a time, the small mining camp of Mammoth Lakes prospered. But unlike her more fortunate neighbor, Bodie; Mammoth's gold was soon exhausted and the frustrated treasure hunters left the Creek and the lakes. They left behind several log cabins and a rusting mill still to be seen in Old Mammoth.

After all these years, Mammoth Lakes is a gold mine of another sort. Immediately after the first good snow, thousands of skiers swarm into the little mountain town. The skiers are mostly from the Los Angeles area, a good six hour drive away. They are the resort's principal income and over a weekend they will spend a great deal of money.

Arriving by car on Friday, wearing brightly colored wool knit caps, mirrored sun glasses and nylon jackets; the skiers quickly fill the motels and condominiums. Rushing to the slopes of Mammoth Mountain, they wait in long lines at the lifts and afterwards, long lines at the dinner houses.

Sunday, bone tired from several days of skiing and partying, they mount their skis to the roof of their cars. All day and late into the night, the weary cars with fogged-up windows — bumper to bumper, begin the long drive back to L.A., their passengers glad to have gotten away for a day or two.

Winter is Mammoth's most profitable season. Summer still draws many vacationers to fish and camp in the mountains. It was in June that Kevin and I first went to Mammoth for a four week gig at Whisky Creek, perhaps the most popular of Mammoth's dinner houses.

Back in Riverside, California, we had just finished six months at another club. In the past five years we had played many of the bars and clubs in the Riverside-San Bernardino area. We had become seasoned musicians and entertainers.

Ironically, what brought me to Mammoth that summer, and what eventually led to the search for Rosa May, was a dream I had had for nearly twenty years: the dream of writing songs and performing them before audiences. That dream had taken a lot of hard, disciplined work, but it had given back some wonderful moments.

It began when I was a kid, when my parents and I visited my grandmother. She had this crippled, old piano. Many of the ivories were gone or cigarette scarred and the finish was wrinkled and cracked like an old man's face. And, it was terribly out of tune. I tinkered with that piano each time we visited my grandmother. I learned to play simple tunes by ear. I remember how I marked the white keys with red nail polish to remember where each song began. The white keys looked awful with the red nail polish but no one cared. It was an old piano.

When I was thirteen, my urge for musical expression suddenly reemerged while listening to Sandy Nelson's, "LET THERE BE DRUMS," a record composed mainly of pounding African rhythms. That record drove my adolescent soul crazy. I wanted to pound drums just like Sandy Nelson.

Deeply inspired, I visited the local music store. I drooled over the glittering red drums displayed in the window. But my hopes fell when I caught the price tag. I would never be a drummer.

I later bought a second-hand guitar for fifteen dollars. I learned to play it by ear and by Mel Bay guitar instruction books.

At fourteen, I was playing lead guitar in a group and making money. I also began writing songs. I played in groups and continued writing music through high school.

For a hyperactive, only child, whose home life was anything but happy, music was an answer. It helped combat the loss of self-esteem caused by an overly strict father, a perfectionist, who continually reminded me how worthless I was. Music helped ease the pain of my parents marital misery. And it helped me survive the loneliness and confusion of seeing my mother crumble before me.

I loved my mother and I felt badly for her. She had always tried so hard to make up for my father's hard ways. And she had paid dearly for that.

My mother had come out of a home life that was filled with horror stories. Her father was a drunk. He often beat his children without reason, kept them awake at night as he howled and pounded walls. There were nights she and her sister lay news-paper on the bedroom floor for a place to urinate. They would not dare venture to the bathroom for fear of being beaten. There were dinner times their father thrust their plates full of food to the floor, Christmases he destroyed their gifts without reason or provo-cation, times he beat their mother in front of them.

Her home life drove my mother to a nervous breakdown at fourteen and to her second when she was sixteen. The emotional scars never healed. My mother was one of those deep feeling, sensitive people who needed tremendous love and understanding.

When I was sixteen, severe depression was causing my mother to sleep eighteen hours a day. My father, consumed by his own emotional problems, never got her to a doctor. My mother eventually cracked-up. My father left her.

Music helped me survive. It brought me friends and attention. It helped me express my anger and my hurt. And it gave me hope. Somewhere down the road was stardom; and with it, I foolishly thought, was the peace of mind, the stability and the reassurance I so desperately needed.

I had studied music three and a half years, left college, then returned to study literature to strengthen my lyric writing. While in college I continued performing in concerts, coffee houses, bars and on radio.

After college, I sang in bars full time. It was a hard, lonely life. It was difficult to sing your heart out through chattering and clinking glasses and a babbling drunk, three feet in front of you. As a bar entertainer, my job was drawing people, making them happy, keeping them drinking. It had little to do with making music. You often felt you were a prostitute and self-respect was difficult to maintain. But playing bars was the way a singer/songwriter made money, until he was well known and drew people to his concerts.

Later, Kevin Lamb and I had teamed up as a duo. We had managed to interest record producers and we were soon to record an album following the gig at Mammoth. At twenty-six, it seemed my dream of becoming a successful singer/songwriter was about to come true.

Chapter 4

Our engagement at Whisky Creek was going well. We worked five nights a week, Wednesday through Sunday, 8:30 to 1:30 A.M. The best nights were Friday through Sunday because of the weekend crowds. Many in our audience were on vacation, happy to be free of their humdrum routines. People were feeling good and in a mood to be entertained which made our work easier and more enjoyable. The Whisky Creek audience was the best we had ever had while working bars. Mammoth, being a resort, had a lot to do with people loosening up. Having audiences that most often listened, applauded and joked back with us raised our confidence and revived our spirits. We tried very hard to give our audiences what they were giving us.

The engagement apparently went well enough and we were asked to continue through July. This meant another month of work and another month to hike and fish in the mountains. If we had not been hired for July, I most likely would have never visited Bodie and become interested in Rosa May's life.

For it was in the first week of July that Kevin and I drove up to nearby Lake Tahoe to see the Smothers Brothers and Neil Sedaka who were then appearing at Harrah's. It was on this trip to Tahoe that I noticed the road sign for Bodie. I had never visited a ghost town before and made a mental note to see Bodie before we left Mammoth.

About a week later I made the hour and a half drive from Mammoth to Bodie. To be specific, the day was July 8, because July 9 is written on the rough draft of **"Rosa May."** And I remember well how the song had nearly written itself the following morning after I'd been out to Bodie. I awoke with the song's melody swimming in my head, finished it in fifteen minutes, and knocked out the lyrics in two hours. The Rosa May song came too easily and from the very start it spooked me.

The day before, I had joggled down the Cottonwood Canyon dirt road into Bodie, over the same road a hundred years earlier, thousands of gold hungry men and women had traveled over. Only they had not ventured to Bodie in a '67 VW Bug, but in thrashing stage coaches; rattling, steel wheeled wagons, by horse and by foot.

I parked beside other visiting cars and campers in the parking area near the Bodie Cemetery. Old cemeteries fascinate me. I love to go through them, searching for the earliest birth and death. The first place I visited was the Bodie cemetery. I noticed how many of the pine markers were empty of names and dates. The hard Bodie weather had blasted away the carved and painted letters. Many graves were overrun with sagebrush which had toppled the surrounding fences.

Leaving the cemetery, I noticed a lone white marker with its back to me. Curious, I crawled under the barbed wire fence.

The marker was Rosa May's and it seemed odd that there were no others near it. Strange too, that her marker was without birth and death years. I stood by her grave for a time. I wondered who Rosa May was and why she was buried out here by herself. The thought came to me that her rugged, lonely marker could be used in a song about Bodie.

I walked down the hill from the cemetery through the sagebrush. I crossed the perimeter road and went through a field where tin cans and glass were strewn about and wagons stood unattended. Along with other tourists I made the self-guided tour through the ghost town, peeking in windows, fascinated. Bodie was once the kind of wild, wicked mining camp, I had seen portrayed in hundreds of westerns. Like many, I wished I could have lived a hundred years earlier and known Bodie when it was the roaring boom camp, full of crazy men and women, when saloons roared day and night and fools battled each other with six-guns.

It was in the Bodie Museum that I learned Rosa May had been a prostitute and for this reason was buried in the outcast cemetery. A rooter of losers, I was immediately curious.

In a glass display case, I found a small black lantern with red glass windows: Rosa May's Red Light. Beside the lantern were various pieces of Victorian clothing and next to these a framed photograph of Rosa May, a pretty girl of about nineteen, with short, dark, curly hair. She was sitting, dressed in a black Victorian gown with long sleeves. There was white lace around the cuffs and the collar of her dress. She sat with her left hand in her lap and there was a bracelet around her left wrist. The right hand curled up, toward her neck, and the delicate fingers held a thin chain that swung from a badge or a medal pinned above her heart. The girl was not smiling nor frowning, her pale face and dark eyes peering at the camera matter of factly. Her eyes showed intelligence and sensitivity and her thin face and delicate hands accentuated the intelligent, sensitive eyes. I studied the century old photograph for several minutes wishing the girl's eyes could explain how such a pretty and delicate young woman ever became a prostitute. There was no need for her to explain to me or anyone else, how she came to live the life she had; still, I was curious.

Beside Rosa's photograph, lay two envelopes; one addressed to her at 18 D Street, the other, 32 South D Street, Virginia City, Nevada. I knew of Virginia City from watching the Bonanza television show for years. Virginia City was another mining camp, though I had no idea when the camp flourished. Rosa May had evidently lived in Virginia City before coming to Bodie.

In the upper right hand corner of each envelope, there was an oval green stamp with the white, embossed figurehead of George Washington. In the upper, curved portion of the stamp above Washington, **U.S. Postage,** was written, and below, **Three Cents.** Over the stamp, a faded blue postmark was stamped but I was unable to read where the letter originated. Each letter had been carried by Wells, Fargo and Co. whose stages were robbed thousands of times in the movies.

I admired how both letters were addressed in the ornate

Victorian script. The letters of each word curled and twisted ever so neatly. Where the writers used little pressure, the lines were thin but where they had pressed hard, the quill had opened wider and allowed more ink to flow onto the paper, making a darker, thicker stroke.

Though Rosa's gravestone did not give her year of death, it occurred to me that a catalog of U.S. stamps could pinpoint the years the green, three cent, stamped envelopes were used. Knowing the years would give me some idea of when Rosa May lived in Virginia City.

(Some weeks later, I learned that the three cent envelope was manufactured by the Plimpton Manufacturing Company at Hartford, Connecticut, and was distributed from 1874 to 1886. Sometime during that twelve year span, Rosa May lived in Virginia City.)

The envelopes did offer one clue to Rosa's character. She had neatly opened each envelope at the narrow, right edge with a sharp letter knife. The knife had cut so clean you had to look closely to see that the edge was slightly torn. One might deduce as an amateur Sherlock Holmes, that Rosa May was a woman of habit who did things rather neatly.

Having wandered through the museum and the rest of the ghost town, fascinated by the old place; I drove back to Mammoth.

All songs begin in the unconscious mind, stimulated and pushed into the conscious mind by a triggering of emotions. Somewhere during my night's sleep, that triggering of emotions had taken place and I awoke, with a simple, folk-like melody playing in my mind. I was quick to make use of my luck.

I lay in bed and listened to the melody, to its rising and falling. When I was certain I had the tune memorized, I boomed out of bed and grabbed my Martin D-28. The battered, old guitar had been with me for five years, through one bad marriage, and the labor pains of over 200 love songs.

The harmony chords to accompany the melody were simple, just four chords: G, A minor, C and D. I noticed immediately that the melody had two basic parts: the melody of the verse and the melody of the chorus. There would be no bridge— no middle section— just verse, chorus; A and B.

I began singing the song and playing a country rhythm to it. I sang la, las and doo-dee-doos for syllable sounds. Gradually, I replaced the syllable sounds with words— any words— to get the feel of what kind of word would sound best with each note. Round open mouth sounds like long O's as in Bo-die, fit best for lower notes. Long E's, as in EE-ZY, sound best on high notes when the throat constricts. I had gone through this word finding process for over twelve years and by this time it was a mechanical, unconscious procedure.

The simplicity of the melody seemed to fit perfectly with Bodie— with its brown, weathered buildings, the sagebrush, its graveyard overrun with weed, with its romance and legends. But it was the image of Rosa May's banished grave and her pretty face that stood out in my mind. And somehow, in that miracle of the creative process, this song came to me and was down on paper within two, intense hours. The rough draft read something like this:

Somewhere in northern California
There's a ghost town the miners once called Bodie
And on a hilltop just outside of Bodie
There stands a stone that simply reads, "Rosa May"

And all the miners who lived back in seventy-nine
Told of her beauty in the saloons and in the mines
Though the women sneered whenever she walked their way
All the miners smiled when they saw Rosa May

Chorus
Rosa May you know I never knew you
But your story's like music to my ears
How you comforted the poor, lonely miners
Can bring a lonesome soul like me to tears

23

Though the miners paid her for her love
She was a woman they always spoke fondly of
A fallen angel with a heart of gold they say
That was the beautiful, the beautiful Rosa May

Chorus
Rosa May you know I never knew you
But your story's like music to my ears
How you comforted the poor, lonely miners
Can bring a lonesome soul like me to tears

Now today, as I walk these streets of Bodie
The miners are gone and the gold has long been spent
The streets are still and the wind whistles through the grass
Buildings brown and burn beneath a hot summer sun

All that's left are the diggings and the mines
Forgotten dreams of thousands of lonely miners
And on a hilltop where the wind blows through the
*   sagebrush*
There stands a stone that simply reads, "Rosa May"

Later, after I had learned more about Rosa's story, I would rewrite the lyrics. The last two verses on the recorded version are different and fit her story better.

After I finished the lyrics, I sang the song over and over. I was pleased with the way it had turned out. There are some songs a writer is closer to than others because he gets more of his guts into them.

"Rosa May" was that kind of song for me, but I did not understand exactly why at first.

The reasons became more apparent later.

The truth is, Rosa May's outcast grave struck a sensitive chord within me. Rosa May was a prostitute. She was different and was ostracized for her difference. She had lived on the outskirts of society. Finally, she was denied burial in the Bodie Cemetery. From the first, that struck me as terribly unfair.

Rosa May's story was something I could genuinely and whole heartedly identify with. Much of my life, I too had felt like an outsider. It had been hard and lonely as a kid feeling I was the cause of my mother and father's marital problems. It seemed that I was always the cause of their arguments. That wasn't really the case but it had seemed so at the time. The arguments had left me feeling terribly guilty. My father's severely critical nature hadn't helped my self-esteem either. In recent years I had begun dealing with the guilt and the lack of self-esteem and I had learned that I wasn't as bad a person as I thought I was. Still, the outsider feelings and past hurts lingered like a sore wound.

I identified with Rosa May for another reason: Rosa May was a prostitute. I had long recognized the fact that I was a prostitute of sorts. I bartered my creative talents in order to survive — to pay bills — to eat. I often worked places where I did not belong. I often entertained people with whom I had little in common, and often, little respect. I did this for money, for it brought me no pleasure. This was simply a fact of life one had to learn to live with. But it was a painful fact that drove you to drink too much and fool yourself too much and do too many crazy things that weren't truly good for yourself or those with whom you did them.

And finally, there was another reason I could identify with Rosa May as an outsider. I was an artist living in a society which respected money, power and success above all things. Successful artists, those who had learned to convert their art into a commercial product — they too were respected. It was the struggling artist who stood between failure and success with whom society did not know how to deal. Such an artist was caught in the, "paying your dues" times. Many American artists had gone through it and many more would be forced to go through it. If you were strong, gifted and lucky; such times would strengthen your courage and determination. But if you lacked nerves of steel — such times could kill you as it had killed many artists before you. That was something you should not think

25

about— especially when far into the dark, lonely night under the depressing influence of alcohol. For you knew self-pity was ultimately self-destructive.

So there was the loneliness, and it was the loneliness which had taken the unknown woman— Rosa May— and unconsciously made her a kind hearted comforter of Bodie's lonely miners. That was how the song had worked. The thought of a kind hearted woman comforting lonely miners somehow comforted me.

Inspired by the Rosa May song, the next day I made another trip to Bodie and once more joggled over the Cottonwood Canyon road. Again I climbed the sage covered hill to Rosa May's grave. Again her misshapen marker seemed to plead for pity. My God, how bad could she have been not to be forgiven in death?

At the Bodie Museum I approached the young woman hired by the State Parks Service there to answer visitor's questions concerning Bodie history.

"Does anyone know anything about Rosa May," I asked, pointing to Rosa's display case.

"Over there," she nodded toward a book rack holding numerous books on Bodie history. "There's a book by Ella Cain," she said. "There's a story in her book about Rosa May." She smiled, "Many are curious about Rosa May." But I didn't want to hear that. I wanted to believe that I was the only one interested in her life.

I picked up the yellow paperback, **The Story of Bodie,** by Ella M. Cain. Born in 1882 in Bodie, Ella Cain was raised in the camp and later taught school there. Over the years she had collected a group of stories she had heard told since childhood. One of these was the story of Rosa May.

Accompanying Cain's story, was a photograph of Rosa May, taken at the age of about twenty-four. In my song I had said Rosa May was beautiful. This photo showed exactly how beautiful she was. With her mouth closed, she smiled innocently at the camera, posing in a long sleeved, black velvet dress. I stared at her for several minutes admiring her beauty, feeling very strange to have written a song about her.

26

Ella Cain's book cost six dollars, I had five on me at the time. Unable to buy the book, I stood and read Cain's seven page, "The Story of Rosa May." Paraphrased, the story goes something like this:

Virgin Alley had a new sign, **The Highgrade,** over the latest house of ill repute on the long street inhabited by the demimonde of the camp. Its occupant was a dark eyed, curly headed, petite French girl. Before coming to Bodie she had lived at 18 South D Street, Virginia City and at No. 1 Ormsby Street, Carson City.

After a very short time in Bodie, Rosa May became the toast and the idol of the men who frequented the sporting district, and there were many. One miner said of her, "She was a gal who had a smile you'd go to hell for and never regret it." Rosa May was the undisputed queen of Bodie's underworld.

Ernest Marks, proprietor of the Laurel Palace Saloon, fell in love with Rosa and she with him. Marks wasn't bad looking, tall and dark with a slight mustache, and true to his Hebrew blood, had inherited the traditional trait of making money. He lavished plenty of it on Rosa in diamonds and furs.

One evening a Cornishman, Billy Owens, attempted to toast Rosa May in Marks' saloon. Marks, easily made jealous, pulled out a gun from under the counter and threatened to use it if Billy or anyone else toasted Rosa. From that time on, bad blood was known to exist between Ernest and Billy.

Shortly afterwards, Rosa took a trip abroad and visited her native Paris. She flitted about Brussels and Berlin and came to a standstill in Monte Carlo. There she gambled away thousands of dollars miners had lost in Ernest's saloon.

Rosa at last returned to Bodie bringing with her ten or fifteen trunks filled with finery and many jewels. She replaced the red lantern that hung on her porch with a fine hand wrought iron one with red panel glass. She also brought silver door knobs, fine furniture and mirrors throughout the house.

While Rosa had been away, the Fortuna Ledge had been discovered in the Standard Mine. Rosa came by a fair share of the highgrade ore miners snuck out of the mine. With this ore she bought more diamonds from Frank Golden, the jeweler. She also had Frank make a pair of cuff links and matchbox from the highgrade. The frames were made of gold and faced with gold-quartz. On the back of the matchbox, E.M. was engraved and below the initials, the figure of a cupid. Rosa gave the matchbox and cuff links to Ernest who was often seen showing them off.

A hard, cold winter hit, deep snows, below zero temperatures, pneumonia weather. A pneumonia epidemic struck the camp. Rosa went from one miner's cabin to another nursing the stricken men. She penned many letters home for the dying men. But the time came when she could no longer go on her mission of mercy. She too had contracted pneumonia. In a few days she was dead. They buried Rosa in the outcast cemetery. Ernest had a picket fence placed around her grave. "Someday," he told himself, "Rosa will have a fitting monument," but the day never came although she left him a fortune in money and diamonds.

Bad luck hit Bodie. The rich Fortuna Ledge faulted and was lost. The boom camp became a ghost town. Only a few old timers held on, Ernest Marks and Billy Owens were two. Over the long years, their feud had healed. Occasionally, the old men played cards to pass the day.

Each day, Ernest's gambling hall and saloon were empty. He lost his fortune and one by one, sold Rosa's jewels far below their worth. Finally there was nothing left to sell but the matchbox and cuff links and a trunk of Rosa's finery and keepsakes that Ernest had treasured all these years.

And now, to make matters worse, Ernest fell into a long lingering illness. Billy Owens was his nurse and companion. Ernest's relatives in New York were notified of his condition. They sent him money until he died. Ernest's last request was to be buried beside Rosa. Billy Owens dug the grave.

In time, Billy Owens died broke. In order to pay for his funeral expenses, the Sheriff auctioned off Billy's lodging house and all its contents. A trunk was brought out and sold. It contained the finery, pictures and letters of Rosa May. Also found, were Ernest's matchbox and gold cuff links, the only items worth anything. The matchbox and cuff links paid for Billy's funeral.

So, Rosa May had comforted dying miners after all, had caught pneumonia and died. Was the story really true or was it simply another romanticized tale of the West?

"I'd take it with a grain of salt," the girl beside the museum door said.

I felt uneasy knowing I had written a song about a woman I knew nothing about and strangely the song had some truth in it. Was it mere coincidence that my ballad of the good hearted whore spun a similar tale to Ella Cain's story, or was there someone out there trying to tell me something, struggling through death and eternity to vindicate herself?

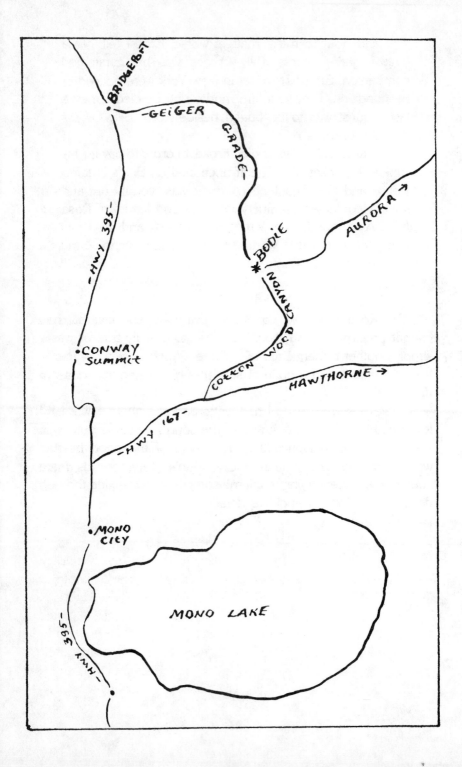

Chapter 5

Seek, and you will find.
— Jesus

I studied the photo of the pretty young woman a consider-
able time each day, seeking a clue to her life's story. I searched
her eyes, her innocent smile, the way she folded her arms, the shape
of her eyebrows, the way she had brushed back her curly, brown
hair showing her ear; noticed too, her dark velvet dress with
three buttons at the elbow, the high collar tight around her neck —
a fashion long outmoded. Little Rosa's shoulders barely
reached the back of a kitchen chair. I wondered what lived
behind her happy eyes, what made her seem so content? Who had
snapped this only photo of her, in what city, what year? Whoever
he was, he had caught Rosa in the spring of her life with his
miracle machine and this image was all that was left of her.

I carried this image of Rosa's pretty face on my many return
trips to Bodie as I walked through the sagebrush to her grave, and
crept over the barren hills surrounding the cluster of rotting
buildings that had been Rosa's last home. During these trips, and
in the months to come, I always tried to imagine what Rosa's life
had been like here in this mining camp.

My imagination soared. Here, in this small valley below, where
tourists wandered with cameras dangling from their necks, entirely
different sights and sounds lived when Rosa was alive. The valley
and the nearby hills had been covered with flimsy buildings.
Children had run through the streets as teams of horses brought
in supplies. Bodie Bluff had been a beehive of activity: men,
horses and wagons went up and down the narrow roads, the ore
wagons filled with rich rock, crept down to the mills with their
burdens, the ore gobbled by wooden shoots and pulverized by
tons of steel. The stamp mills, yes — and the Standard Mill still

standing at the foot of Bodie Bluff, they had pounded day and night, their roaring had filled the valley, the white smoke had climbed upward out of the tall, black stacks into the blue sky. Men had struggled and prayed the rich Fortuna vein would hold out so that prosperity would continue. Men, rich and poor, had raced through the streets speaking excitedly of this new strike in this or that mine. The stage came and went, saloons roared day and night, men gambled at poker tables, men gambled with Bodie stocks, prostitutes gambled with their lives. And it was all gone, lost behind the veil of time, the life Rosa had lived, the sights and sounds she had taken for granted. Now here I was on a hill, looking down on a gathering of weathered buildings, reaching with my imagination, my questions and my theories. Could I ever really know what life was like here in Bodie?

In my mind, Rosa's eyes stared steadily into mine.

Was it possible for any woman — even a prostitute — to be happy living in such a reckless and wild a place as Bodie, with hundreds of whisky-mouthed men, pounding her door night and day, anxious to go down into the heat of her tiny body for as long as she would permit? Could this kind of life make any woman happy or was this simply a means of living, something Rosa was doing in the meantime, until something better came along? Or was Rosa like other whores who fooled themselves, believing someday, some wonderful man would come along and sweep them away from the hell they lived? There were so many questions, so much I wanted to know and didn't.

I walked alone through a large open field at the far north end of Bodie. Cattle grazed there, blackbirds twittered in the grass. Few tourists wandered this field as I did. They were not aware that Chinatown and the Bodie red light had once stood here.

The Chinese had lived on King Street, which ran off Main Street. Here they built their joss houses and opium dens, and from here carted their vegetables uptown. Bonanza Street, or Virgin Alley as it was most often called, sprouted north from King Street and ran the length of the field just behind and parallel to Main Street. Back doors of the Main Street saloons emptied the miners directly into the red light. Here along Bonanza Street, the row of cribs stood, small frame shacks where the prostitutes lived and worked. The cribs and their women, the Chinese and the saloons, were all gone. Part of Chinatown burned down in the 1932 fire that wiped out seventy percent of Bodie. The remaining buildings were later torn down. Chinatown's inhabitants had left behind their heaps of trash, rusting tins, busted bottles violet with age, square holes now being eaten up by summer grass where outhouses once stood. You could just barely see a slight indentation running through the field where Bonanza Street once was. It was many years since that road carried a man "down the line."

My mind wandered on. In summer, those girls who were not busy with customers, would have come out of their cribs in the late afternoon to sit on their stoops, casting their sleepy eyes toward Bodie Bluff, watching the thick-backed men, very aware that their coming and going put the bread in their bellies and the gold in their purses. There would be name calling and threats and laughter among the women. One or two would already be drunk. Others would defiantly wait for the shriek of the shift whistle.

Some of the women were young and pretty like Rosa May and some were old and beaten. Many were unhappy and reckless, a matter of time before they did themselves in. Yet each woman knew this: Bodie was a mining camp with many men and few women. Money can be made from man's need for woman. These women were whores but were needed here as much as the men who worked the hot depths of Bodie Bluff.

But of all the women who had lived and worked in this field I now walked, only one was still remembered, one honored, one spoke of among tourists and neighboring residents. It was Rosa May. And why? Because a legend had grown up around her name, a story of a kind hearted whore who died while nursing miners. Word of mouth, generation after generation, had made Rosa a saint. Ella Cain furthered this legend with her account of Rosa May. All who had spoken well of Rosa expressed their child-like faith in the inherent goodness of legends, of vague people who lived long ago and did wonderful things. Who could think

33

badly of Rosa now, even if she was a whore? She had died a martyr legend claimed. Now romance surrounded her name and people wanted to believe their romantic notions. For Rosa's story flavored Bodie's bygone days with sentiment.

As I sang "Rosa May" in the Whisky Creek bar, weekenders fastened their ears to every word. Without fail, someone would come up during breaks, with eager eyes, hungry to know more about Rosa May, a "lady of the evening." I was made aware that I was not alone in my curiosity.

The idea of a book about Rosa's life began to bob in the back of my mind. To write such a book would require a great deal of research. It would also take a lot of time and money. I could make the time but money would be a real problem.

There was another problem. I had never made a historical research. How and where was one to begin?

One could start with people. Locate old-timers who had lived in Bodie and possibly known Rosa May or something about her. At this time, I believed that Rosa May died around 1880 as her marker vaguely claimed. The chances of finding anyone alive who might have known Rosa were slim. Still, there was a chance.

Second, there were books. I had read Ella Cain's, **The Story of Bodie,** and noticed several other books about Bodie in the Bodie Museum. Through these I might discover more about Rosa May.

Third, old newspapers of the era might also provide information. If Rosa May had been well known, my chances of finding items on her were good. If she had not been famous, research would be more difficult. Certainly something about her would show up if I searched hard and long enough.

And fourth, public records might also provide facts about Rosa's life. Bodie being within Mono County, records for Bodie would most likely be found at Bridgeport, Mono County seat.

It was now mid-July. Kevin and I would be at Whisky Creek until August 1. Following this, we had a week engagement near Lake Tahoe. I figured I had about three weeks in the Bodie area to research before heading south to record our album.

In her story, Ella Cain provided some information on Rosa May. I planned to check this information out. Most of this could be done at the Bridgeport courthouse where death and land records are kept. I hoped something would turn up regarding Rosa May, Ernest Marks and Billy Owens.

As the two lane highway winds down from Conway Summit, you enter a wide green valley two hours north of Mammoth. Just outside of town you pass cattle grazing in the moist fields and water in ditches beside the road. Blackbirds dangle from barbed wire fences. The air smells warm and earthy from the water and the moist fields. This would be a nice place to live. The wide valley feels calm. The little settlement of Bridgeport rests here quietly beside the East Walker River, with the dark Sierras, some still patched with snow, to the east. The town is no more than a block long, with several restaurants and motels. If you blink, you might pass Bridgeport, head into the mountains and go north to Carson City. Somehow the pioneer settlement of Bridgeport has managed to survive while the nearby boom camps of Bodie, Masonic and Lucky Boy have come and gone.

The most conspicuous building in Bridgeport is the two story wooden courthouse, snow white and trimmed in bright red, built in 1880, the second year of Bodie's boom. The Bridgeport people take excellent care of the old courthouse and do not permit pigeons to roost in the high nooks below the roof. Chicken wire protects these places from their would-be messy inhabitants.

My first objective was to discover when Rosa May died. Knowing her time of death, I could limit research to the years preceding. Time of death would also help determine how feasible it was to locate people who knew Rosa May.

I was excited as I walked to the county clerk's office down the halls of high ceilings and rich hard woods. I explained to an elderly, grey haired lady what I was doing. She kindly led me to a huge vault, its thick steel door stood open. Inside the vault were stacks of old leather bound volumes, you could smell their years inside the musty vault. The clerk explained that the deceased would be listed in an index. There were several indexes, each covering so many years. I was limiting my search at this point, between 1865-1900. I thought this to be a fair span. Once I found the name I was looking for, beside the name would be a volume and a page number which would contain the actual death certificate.

When searching for ownership of land, there were similar indexes. These were called Grantor-Grantee indexes, the grantor, being the seller; the grantee, the buyer.

The clerk left the vault and I opened the index of deaths to the M section. As I ran my finger down the long column of names, struggling to read the ornate Victorian script, I discovered that the names were in absolutely no alphabetical order. What should have been a simple task had now become an ordeal of going down column after column, page after page of names.

I spent an entire morning searching the indexes of death and land records. I did not find a single reference to Rosa May. As far as Mono County records went, Rosa May had never owned land nor died in Bodie. Evidently a negligent physician years ago failed to notify authorities of Rosa's death or perhaps authorities hadn't cared to list the death of a prostitute. Then again, I had recently learned of two disastrous fires in Bodie, in 1892 and 1932. Perhaps a death record at Bodie was destroyed in one of these fires. But county clerks assured me, all of Bodie's public records had always been kept at Bridgeport. If Rosa May died in Bodie, county records should bear proof. But they didn't.

I left the courthouse and walked to a nearby hamburger stand. I filled my knawing stomach with a barbecue beef and a large root beer. If county records showed nothing, how would I learn anything substantial about her life? Fortunately, Ella Cain mentioned in her story the names of Ernest Marks, Rosa's lover, and Billy Owens. I gobbled my lunch, rested my eyes, and went back to work.

During the afternoon, I managed to gather the first bits of information regarding Rosa May, Ernest Marks and Billy Owens.

The first record I found on Ernest Marks was a land transaction. He had sold lot 52 of block 21 in Bodie to Charles Kuhlman for twenty dollars June 13, 1898. I was very surprised to find the year 1898. I had figured that Rosa, Ernest and Billy had died before this. Not so. In fact, Ernest Marks' death certificate states he died July 28, 1928, from heart failure and chronic prostatitis. Born in Prussia in 1853, Marks was seventy-five at death. The certificate made it clear, that Billy Owens, the undertaker, buried Ernest in the Odd Fellows Cemetery. Here was the first discrepency between Ella Cain's account and county records. I later learned that the Odd Fellows Cemetery was located inside the regular Bodie cemetery. If Billy had buried Ernest inside the fence, then Ernest was not buried beside Rosa in the outcast cemetery as Ella Cain claimed. Also, while last in Bodie, I had made a point of checking this out and found that there was no evidence of another grave beside Rosa's — no marker, no mound of dirt, no grave. I was inclined to believe that Rosa was buried in the outcast cemetery by herself, that Ella Cain had simply let her imagination go to give her story a sentimental ending. I was beginning to question Cain's diligence.

Billy Owens' death certificate states he was born April 7, 1855 in Missouri. He died September 4, 1933 in Bodie from a heart attack. Billy had lived in the Bodie area for fifty years. He worked in the mines, became an undertaker and later, Justice of the Peace. His mother was A.J. Johnson.

Land records revealed that Billy had owned lots 23 and 24 of block 11 in Bodie. This property, the buildings, and all within were sold at a Sheriff's auction July 25, 1934, to pay for Billy's funeral just as Ella Cain said in her story. A certain B.C. Honea had purchased Billy's property for $50.

At the mention of Billy's property, I remembered that Ella Cain had spoke of a certain trunk that once belonged to Rosa which had been sold after Rosa's death. Her trunk, which contained clothing, photos and letters; came into Ernest's keeping and later fell into Billy's hands when Ernest died. I figured if I found B.C. Honea, whoever he was and if he was still alive, I might find the letters that had once belonged to Rosa May. Such letters could provide first hand information about her life. They were invaluable. I would have to locate B.C. Honea. Chances were, he was still in the area.

For now, I was through with county records. I walked out of the musty vault into the bright July sun. My eyes ached, my head throbbed. A little tired but my mind was on fire. I must somehow find a lead on someone who could provide specific information about Rosa May. I was pleased that I had learned something about Ernest Marks and Billy Owens. That they had died as late as 1928 and 1933 was encouraging. I might after all find someone still alive who had known Rosa May.

My next thought was the Mono County Museum. Perhaps the museum might have books or information about Rosa May. The curator might also provide leads on old-timers who had lived in Bodie.

I raced over to the museum and quickly went through its numerous exhibits seeking two words: Rosa May. I did find a colored print of a middle aged woman in a dress that looked as if it might have been worn in the 1890's. The type written note said the print was of Rosa May, a Bodie hurdy-gurdy girl of the 1880's and 90's. I doubted the print was of Rosa May. It looked nothing like her other photos, but I wanted to know who at the museum knew about Rosa living in Bodie in the 1890's.

At the entrance, I found a thin, middle aged man, bent over a large canvas. He was painting a Western scene of a prairie schooner and sagebrush in water colors. He hardly noticed me staring at him while he worked. He dipped his brush into the colors, made a tiny stroke on the canvas, dipped the brush in clean water, then back into the colors again. I thought I should not disturb him, then remembered what little time was left before I had to return to Southern California.

I introduced myself and told the painter what I was looking for. Keeping a keen eye on his work, the painter told me he was the curator of the museum. He was busy and I could see he didn't want to be bothered but I figured he could help me if I kept at him.

I asked the curator about Ella Cain's story of Rosa May. He had known Ella, she was dead now. I was sorry. I had many questions to ask her. I explained that Ella did not include dates in her story. Ella wasn't particular when it came to dates, he answered. I wondered if she was very diligent with other details. As far as he knew, Ella's story of Rosa May was true. And the print of Rosa May in the museum, where had that come from? Someone had donated it, he didn't know who. Who said Rosa was a hurdy-gurdy girl in the 1890's? He didn't know.

I began to ask him about his painting, how long he had been at it, whether or not it had brought him financial gain. At my interest in his work, the painter perked up. He had been painting quite a long while and his paintings had earned large sums. Some of his paintings were in various museums.

I wasn't the first one who had searched for information regarding Rosa May. I was stung with jealously. I wanted to believe that I was the only one who cared a damn about her life. Not so. There were many who had searched for the details of her life. I would find nothing he warned me, so far no one had. But for all it was worth, there was an old man, Bill Glenn, who used to work around the museum and had always spoken well of Rosa May. Bill Glenn was born in Bodie but he lived in Oakland now. Perhaps he might help me. The curator gave me the address and I thanked him.

I drove back to Mammoth, content to have found something. I would write Bill Glenn and see what he had to say.

In the weeks that followed, I read several books about Bodie. Though quite informative as to the history of Bodie and mining camp life, they only mentioned Rosa May in passing.

End of July and our gig at Whisky Creek was at an end. The mountains were beautiful and the weekenders who listened to our music had brought us much happiness. We would miss them and several of the new friends we had made.

It was time to go. We filled my VW and Kevin's squeaking Toyota with amplifiers and guitars and headed up 395 toward Tahoe. At our next club we were given a cabin and meals, plus our regular wages. The nights came and went, we met new faces but we would be gone soon. The loneliness of life without roots nagged us.

In this final week in the area, I made one more trip to Bridgeport. You may remember that Rosa's marker was made by a man called Serventi. He had written his name at the base of the marker. I figured Serventi had known Rosa and may have lived near her in Chinatown. I planned to check this out by going through land records.

In the Bridgeport courthouse, I found a deed dated October 6, 1890, which stated that a certain Antonio Serventi, sold lots 26 and 30 of block 26. Block 26 was the red light area and lots 26 and 30 were about a hundred feet behind Virgin Alley. Antonio Serventi was a neighbor of Rosa's. Had he made her marker?

In the phone book I found a Louis Serventi in Bishop. Figuring there was a slight chance Louis was related to Antonio Serventi, I gave him a call. An aged, raspy voice answered the phone. It was Louis Serventi and he spoke with a thick Italian accent.

"Mr. Serventi?"

"Yesa."

"My name is George Williams. I'm doing research on Rosa May of Bodie. Was Antonio Serventi a relative of yours?"

"He was my uncle. He dead a long time. Die in the twenties." I couldn't believe my luck.

"He lived in Bodie in the 1890's?"

"Yesa. He come to America from the old country. Then go to the gold strikes in Colorado, then come to Bodie. I remember him telling us children stories about Bodie."

"Did he ever mention Rosa May?"

"Ah ... No, he never menshun Rosie May."

"Her gravestone has Serventi written on it. I think Antonio might have made it for her."

"No, Uncle Antonio not make Rosie's marker. I make it."

"**You** made it!"

"Yesa. I make it long time ago."

"When?"

"Les see… I still had the Jeep. Maybe 1965 or so."

"Why did you make it for her? Did you know Rosa May?"

"No, I not know Rosie May. She a good woman. I read about her in the book."

"What book?"

"Uh…"

"You scribbled 1880 on her marker. How do you know she died in 1880?"

"The book say so."

"The Ella Cain book?"

"Yesa, I think so."

There were no dates in Ella's story.

"Look Mr. Serventi, this is long distance. I can't keep it any longer. I'll write you a letter. You've been very helpful." I hung up and copied his address out of the phone book.

When I finally visited Louis Serventi in Biship, I found him a very kind man of 83, his thick white hair combed straight back, a deep brown nose drooping over his lip. He had been wrong about Rosa's year of death. His error opened the possibility that Rosa might have died years later. Perhaps, I kept wishing, there was someone still alive who had known her.

Louis Serventi lived in a large house surrounded by flowers with a daughter who had been mentally crippled by spinal meningitis . I couldn't believe it when he introduced us.

"This is Rosa," he said.

Kevin and I drove our cars back down 395, past Bridgeport, Mammoth and Bishop. We crossed the hot Mojave desert at night, the warm August air in through the windows, you smelled the dryness of the land. As we neared San Bernardino, there was the stink of smog. I'd been away from smog for two months breathing fresh mountain air. Now the smell was repulsive. We left the high

Mojave desert and weaved down the Cajon pass into San Bernardino. The smog grew thicker the closer we came to San Bernardino, one of the most severely polluted cities in the world.

A friend of ours had recently married and I was to watch his house while he honeymooned. This worked out perfectly. I was planning to move nearer to Hollywood as soon as possible and I didn't want to hassle looking for a temporary apartment.

While house-sitting, I began work on a novel about Rosa May. I had to exercise quite a bit of imagination because I knew very little about her life. After working out a frustrating first chapter, it was evident that I would have to know more about Rosa's life to write a novel.

Fortunately, our record producer was busy with another project which would keep him busy until September. That left plenty of time to go back to the Bodie area to do more research.

Before leaving for Bridgeport, I wrote Bill Glenn in Oakland and Louis Serventi in Bishop.

Bill Glenn was quick to reply. Born in 1899, Bill Glenn was 77. He remembered Rosa May, Ernest Marks and Billy Owens from his childhood. He recalled Rosa giving dimes to children in the street. He could not remember what she looked like. He remembered Ernest Marks as a small man who was lame and had the gout. Billy Owens was "just a regular guy" who did odd jobs and later became Bodie's undertaker.

Of the three, Rosa died first, he didn't know exactly when. Marks, he claimed, was buried beside her. He thought much of what he remembered might have been things he overheard his parents say. He believed Ella's story about Rosa dying while helping miners. He said, at that time in Bodie, there was great fear of epidemics of pneumonia, scarlet fever and diphtheria as these diseases took many lives.

In reply to a question about a town paper, Bill said the Bodie Miner, published papers up until 1908-09. Jim Nugent, publisher and editor, took over the Bridgeport Chronicle-Union when the Bodie Miner folded.

This was about all Bill Glenn knew. He urged me to talk with

Stuart and Sadie Cain in Bridgeport, who would know more.

Louis Serventi's reply explained more specifically, that Antonio came to America in his early twenties, headed for the Colorado gold strikes and later came to Bodie, where he worked at the Mono Mills, a lumber outfit about thirty miles south of Bodie on the southeast shore of Mono Lake.

Louis Serventi had known an old man who was a friend of Rosa's and Ernest Marks. The old man said that Ernest **was** buried beside Rosa. Before the old man died, he asked Louis to make Rosa May a marker. As luck would have it, the old man was now dead.

As a child of eight or nine, Bill Glenn would have seen Rosa around 1908. With Billy Owens and Ernest Marks dying as late as 1928 and 1933, I felt there was a very good chance, someone was still alive who had known Rosa May.

In the night, I loaded my VW bug with sleeping bag, Coleman stove, lantern, fuel and a cooler full of food and drink. I headed up the Cajon pass, over the Mojave desert, back to Bodie hoping to find the man or woman who long ago was Rosa's friend.

Chapter 6

As I sped down the dark, two lane desert highway toward Bishop, I had plenty of time to consider what I was doing. Strange how suddenly my thoughts were taken up with a mining camp prostitute. A month before, I couldn't have imagined driving hundreds of miles seeking the story of a life lived years before I was thought of. And yet, here I was, in the middle of the desert, obsessed enough to spend my last two hundred dollars in the hope of finding answers. I had no idea what I would do when the money was gone or where I'd live when I returned to Riverside. Somehow, things would work out.

Like every American kid, I had been raised on t.v. westerns. All I knew about the wild West was learned watching television. So I knew very little. Nor did I know much about mining camps nor mining camp prostitutes except what I'd recently read. So it was easy for me to have romantic notions of the West's earlier days and the life of this Rosa May. Her story in itself was romantic enough, blurred by just enough years to make it seem a fairy tale. Buried in those distant years and in Rosa's vague story, was a real woman who had lived a life, in some ways, very different from mine. I longed to touch that life for it had been lived in a romantic and fascinating era that I would never be able to live in despite modern technology.

So there I was, a modern Don Quixote, speeding over the warm Mojave desert in a VW bug, the warm alkaline air blowing my long hair back, trying my best to ride right into Rosa May's past life. Over desert and mountain I was coming to Rosa's defense, hoping to unearth her life from years of misquoted stories and distorted facts. With my sword-like pen, I would tell her

45

true story, the story I now imagined of a woman whose life had gone sadly astray. For at this time, Rosa May was no ordinary whore to me. Her martyr death had redeemed an otherwise ugly life, and its compassionate end, made her life as a whore more palatable to myself and the thousands of grandmas who visit Bodie each year.

I promised myself I would do whatever I could to discover the truth of Rosa's life. If her life in reality was the legend Ella Cain told of, I would be content. Like many of Rosa's believers, I too wanted to think the best of her. There was, of course, the possibility research might prove that Ella's tale was a mere fabrication, that Rosa May had simply been a plain mining camp whore. I was tampering with a legend, one many would like to believe. They wouldn't think kindly of me if I proved the legend they had taken to heart was a lie.

I laid these thoughts aside. I was becoming too tired. I switched on the radio to keep awake. I found a country music station which pleased me. Somehow country music and dark desert highways fit perfectly.

In the early morning hours I had gone over most of the Mojave desert and was now driving beneath the Sierras. I smelled the fresh water in the air and the damp, clean smell of wet sagebrush. The highway gleamed from a brief desert shower. I wanted to make Bishop, but now very tired, I would settle for Independence, 42 miles south.

I was bone tired when I reached Independence. I pulled off at a rest area and drove down a dirt road lined with trucks and campers. I parked far from the noise of the highway. I laid a ground cloth on the dirt and crawled into my sleeping bag. I went right to sleep. In less than four hours the sun would be blazing.

By 6:30 the desert sun was roaring down upon my nylon sleeping bag making it impossible to sleep any longer. I wrapped the bag up, threw it in the car and with tired eyes drove the remaining miles to Bishop. In Bishop I grabbed a quick breakfast and drove over to Louis Serventi's. I planned to interview him again and try to jog his memory on a few details.

It had been many years since Louis' friend died, the old man who had known Ernest Marks and Rosa. Louis tried hard to remember his name. It might have been Mike or John, he wasn't certain. It was too far back for him to recall. But Louis did offer me the addresses of his cousins, Margherita and Louise, the daughters of Antonio Serventi.

Louise and Margherita, ladies in their seventies, talked for an hour and a half about their father, Antonio. They brought out an old photo album of Antonio's, the red velvet covering now worn with handling, the figure of an antlered buck embossed on the cover. We three went through the old photos together, me hoping to find another photo of Rosa May. Very unlikely, but worth a try.

Antonio was a warm, charitable man, a laborer with a fine gift for storytelling. Louise and Margherita had listened many hours to Antonio's tales of Bodie and other mining camps. Born in 1852, he sailed from Italy to New York in his early twenties, made his way to Colorado searching for gold, then came to California. The ladies could not recall Antonio telling them what years he had been in Bodie. They thought it was after the boom years. They were surprised when I told them Antonio had owned land behind the Bodie red light in the 1890's. He had never mentioned owning land in Bodie.

They explained that Antonio had worked at the Mono Mills and later made charcoal for use in the Bodie mines. He left Bodie when Tonopah, Nevada boomed in the early 1900's. He later moved to Big Pine where he met his wife, Marie. He was forty-eight when he married. Eventually, Antonio and Marie moved to Bishop where Antonio built their home and farmed on six acres.

Unfortunately, but to be expected, the ladies could not remember Antonio ever speaking of Rosa May. I was certain he had known Rosa May, perhaps had even spent a few dollars on her. With Antonio dying in 1920, many answers went with him. I thought it quite an irony how Louis Serventi, seventy years later, had made Antonio's neighbor, Rosa May, a grave marker.

For now, I was done in Bishop. I was eager to climb out of the hot valley to the cooler mountains and on to Bodie. As I drove up the steep incline to the mountains, my engine began giving me trouble. I had had the engine rebuilt two months earlier. I had been warned the engine might last a month or a year. I angrily figured the engine wasn't going to last long and I had little money with me to have it fixed if it broke down. I was worried but I would go on. I prayed that the car would hold together until I got back to Riverside.

It was good to be in the mountains again. With my mind busy figuring out ways to learn more about Rosa's life, the two and a half hour drive to Bodie seemed to fly. I passed Mammoth and Lee Vining and circled Mono Lake. Years ago, the Mono Mills had sawed timber on the lake's southeastern shore. It was there Antonio worked. From 1881 to 1917 a light guage railroad ran from Mono Mills around the eastern shore and north over the mountains to Bodie. The train twisted up steep switchbacks and arrived on top of Bodie Bluff. It was not a passenger train but used instead to haul 'uuge quantities of wood used in the stamp mills and in the miners' cottages. Chinese woodcutters also gathered wood in the nearby hills and hauled it to Bodie on squads of burros. They sold the wood to the mills and to the townspeople who were always afraid of a wood famine. If there was no wood, the mills could not operate and men could not work.

In Bodie I once more walked the haunted streets and the field where Rosa had lived and died, then up the hill to her grave. There I paused for a moment, wishing she might speak or a major relevation would come. None came. I walked back down the hill, passing many tourists, remembering how a month earlier I had first visited Bodie.

In the Bodie Museum I reexamined Rosa's photograph, the pieces of clothing, and the envelopes addressed to her. The envelopes caught my attention. Perhaps there were return addresses and names on the backs of the envelopes. Names and addresses could certainly help me. I asked the girl who watched over the museum if she would turn the envelopes over. She looked at me strangely and refused. Disappointed, I left the museum.

On Main Street I noticed a blond middle aged woman dressed in a long Victorian dress, her hair neatly pinned up in the 1890's fashion. She was Ardie Adkisson, wife of Bob Adkisson, head park ranger. I introduced myself and explained what I was doing. Ardie Adkisson was a Rosa May enthusiast; we hit it off.

My first leads to old-timers came from Ardie who had met several on their occasional visits to Bodie to reminisce. From one elderly gentleman, Ardie heard that Rosa had fallen in love with a gambler, a real low-life. Another old-timer said Rosa May had been a madam in five mining camps: Virginia City, Bodie, Masonic, Lundy and Columbia.

In the nearby area there were several old-timers who might be able to help me. Ardie gave me their names and addresses.

In Bishop, there was Richie Conway, who lived in Bodie as a kid and knew a lot about Bodie's early days. In Smith Valley, there was a Mrs. Bell, in her nineties, who had lived in Bodie for years. Her son, Bob Bell, was out in Luning, Nevada. Bob Bell knew a lot about Bodie's early days but he was shy.

Ardie had also met the niece of an old chinaman, who in earlier days, drove stage between Bodie and Hawthorne, Nevada. Ardie gave me the niece's address.

In Mono City, there was Frank Balfe who seemed to know a great deal about Rosa May. Ardie gave me directions.

I explained to Ardie about the return addresses on Rosa's envelopes. She too was curious. We went back into the museum and Ardie opened the locked display case. Turning the envelopes over, there were no names or addresses. We were disappointed.

As I drove to nearby Mono City to interview Frank Balfe, I wondered if Rosa May really was a madam of five mining camps, or whether she had fallen in love with a gambler as Ardie heard. I would hear lots of stories. I would have to carefully sift them to find the truth.

In Mono City, I found Frank Balfe's house with no trouble; Ardie gave me good directions.

In the last ten years, Frank Balfe had taken a genuine interest in the Rosa May legend and had managed to gather some good information. Most of this came from Father Birks, an old man who served as a watchman at Bodie for several years. Father Birks was supposedly a priest and Bodie was one of his first parishes. Frank had met Birks in the late 1950's on a trip to Bodie. Birks was dead now, buried in the Bodie cemetery.

Father Birks remembered Rosa May as an older woman, about 57 or 60. I was surprised to hear this. I had imagined Rosa dying young, still quite pretty. Not so, according to Birks.

She had come from some place back east. Birks thought it was upstate New York. She had worked five or seven years in fancy brothels in Carson and Virginia City. She had spent the majority of time in Carson City though she made trips to Bodie where she also lived. In Bodie, she married a rich miner in later years. Birks could not remember the man's name. Thought it was a short Anglo-Saxon name with five or six letters.

Having known Rosa well himself, Birks said she was indeed a good hearted woman, something many said of her. Birks recalled old man Scanivino. The Scanivinos lived for years at the Goat Ranch, nine miles south of Bodie on Cottonwood Canyon road. Old man Scanivino had known Rosa May. He had nothing but good to say about her. Scanivino, too, was now buried in the Bodie cemetery.

Father Birks believed Rosa died in Carson City. As she had requested, her body was brought back to Bodie for burial. I wondered if this was the reason I was unable to find a record of death.

The townspeople would not allow Rosa to be buried in the regular cemetery. Nor would they allow her grave to be marked. Surprisingly, they did allow her husband burial inside the fence. This was about all Birks knew about Rosa May.

Frank Balfe had one last bit of information. Several years ago while visiting the Bodie Museum, he saw a letter that Rosa May had written. It was in one of the display cases.

Frank could not recall to whom the letter was written but it was clear that Rosa was writing from Carson City to someone in Bodie. In the letter she said she had not been feeling well, that she had a cold or the chills. Frank could not remember the date the letter was written but he stressed that it was from Carson City.

When Frank last visited Bodie, he was disturbed when he discovered Rosa's letter missing from the glass display case. Elaine Bell, Bob Bell's wife, was curator of the museum at the time. I should ask Elaine about the letter. Frank stressed that the letter did exist.

I drove back to Bodie and searched the cemetery for Birks' grave. I found it. The marker read: Father Clarence C. Birks, 1897-1961, "Watchman" 1958-61. Because of his late birth, I doubted Birks ever knew Rosa May. If Bodie was one of his first parishes, it could not have been so until the 1920's. I later learned that the Catholic church had pulled out of Bodie by 1909. My suspicions concerning Birks were confirmed the next day by Bob Bell in Luning, Nevada.

From Bodie I drove sixty miles out into the Nevada desert to Hawthorne. It was early evening when I arrived. Too tired for another interview, I hung around the various gambling halls watching those more confident in their luck lose their wallets over the green felt tables. Bored and tired, I headed towards Luning, twenty-five miles east of Hawthorne. I pulled off the road somewhere between Hawthorne and Luning, spread my sleeping gear on the dirt and spent a restless night listening to the lullabies of diesel trucks as they roared and rumbled down the highway into miles and more miles of desert.

The hot desert sun woke me early and I drove the remaining miles to Luning, nothing more than a gas station, a bar and a tiny cluster of houses. At a roadside rest area I fixed some eggs and bacon and at 9 sharp I was pounding on the door of Bob and Elaine Bell's mobile home.

Fortunately, the Bell's were early risers. The door opened and

Elaine Bell, a tall, outgoing, middle aged woman met me. I told her who I was and what I was doing. She asked me in and I met Bob Bell. Bob was about the same age, dressed in mechanics overalls, with wonderful impish eyes. He was, as Ardie said, a little shy but he seemed glad to answer my questions about Bodie.

Bob was born and raised in Bodie and was familiar with some of the town's stories. Unfortunately, he was born years after Rosa May's death but he did know something about her.

He figured Rosa May came to Bodie in the camp's later years, perhaps the 1890's. He remembered Ernest Marks and him being crippled with rheumatism. Marks kept his saloon open until he died but he ended up broke.

Bob laughed when I mentioned Billy Owens. Owens was a funny little old man who was into everyone's business. Billy's mother, Grandma Johnson, ran a boarding house. Billy inherited the place when his mother died.

Bob couldn't recall hearing the story of Rosa dying while nursing miners. Nor could he recall hearing about the feud between Billy Owens and Ernest Marks over Rosa.

Besides Rosa, there was another prostitute in Bodie, Emma Goldsmith. Emma, like Rosa, was a madam, but of the two houses, it seemed Emma's was more popular.

Bob figured Rosa May must have died in the 1890's.

I asked Elaine Bell about the missing Rosa May letter. Elaine said there never was such a letter. She also said that the clothing in the museum which is supposed to be Rosa May's, was in fact Dolly Cains, Jim Cain's daughter.

And about Father Birks, my suspicions were quickly confirmed. Bob Bell knew Birks personally and said, "Birks was no more a priest than you or I." Birks was married and before coming to Bodie he and his wife had lived in Bishop. If Birks had lied about being a priest, he could have lied about what he told Frank Balfe. But I later learned that much of what Birks told Frank Balfe is true.

I believe much of Birks' information came from Ella Cain. It was the Cain family who had hired Birks as a Bodie watchman.

During the three years he was watchman, Ella Cain was setting up the Bodie Museum. Ella and Birks had obviously talked about Rosa May.

It was during these talks that Ella Cain passed on information only she knew. For it was Ella, I would later learn, who had found the Rosa May letters when Billy Owens' property was auctioned off. B.C. Honea had bought Billy's property. Ella had bought Rosa's trunk, full of clothing, photographs and personal letters. Ella had read the letters, some twenty-six, and learned the truth of Rosa's life. Some of this she told Birks, who with his wild imagination, distorted the facts here and there and finally imagined himself a personal acquaintance of Rosa's.

But I did not know this when I left Bob and Elaine Bell and drove across the desert back to Bishop. My mind whirled with all I had recently heard about Rosa's life. I didn't know what to believe.

It was then that I became aware of a strange presence riding with me in the car. I felt something was pointing the way, opening doors, and would lead me to the truth. Something peculiar was happening, I felt it but I could not make sense of it, yet it was there near me. Something was going to turn up, something definite about Rosa's life.

And then the car began falling apart. At fifty it would backfire and lose power. I figured the heads were loosening. Two months ago I had paid two hundred and fifty dollars to have the engine rebuilt and now this. I was furious.

I stopped the car and lifted the hood up. I spit on the engine. The spit sizzled. The engine was overheating and if I wasn't careful it would blow up and I'd be stuck in the Nevada desert. I let the engine cool down, hopped in and drove eighty miles to Bishop.

In Bishop I found Richie Conway's house on the north edge of town. His farmhouse door was wide open but he was gone and stayed gone as long as I waited.

It was about six in the evening and Bishop was still very hot. After driving all day, asking strangers questions and the car giving me trouble, I was frazzled. My money would last only so long. I couldn't keep this trip more than seven days and I was already into the third, and I wanted to learn so much more. And now Richie Conway wasn't home.

I drove down East Line Street and just before the bridge I turned right onto a dirt road and drove a half mile along the river. I remembered this place I'd been to before, it was an open spot beside the river, nice and grassy. Here the Owens River was only twenty feet across.

I undressed and slid into the river. The freezing water, fresh out of the Sierras, sent shocks up my body. I found a shallow spot, bathed and got out.

Early evening but the sun was still hot. A hot breeze quickly dried my naked body. I shaved, using the outside car mirror. With my face smooth and white, plenty of B.O. Juice under my arms, I felt clean and refreshed.

I pulled the Coleman stove out of the trunk, pumped it, lit it up. I emptied a can of beans into a saucepan, cut up hot dogs and dropped them in. Seven minutes, dinner was ready. I dished the meal out, poured some cold milk, sat down and leaned against the fender. I listened to the green water as it gurgled and calmly pushed against the river banks. In the trees, birds sang to their lovers. The smell of fresh water and cool, greenery swelled within me. The river pushed against the banks. A tight feeling came into my throat. Exhaustion swept over me. My life at that moment seemed like an ocean without shores. The river I listened to at least had banks to push against. I too longed for someone to lean against. A man hates to admit it, but he needs boundaries. Without them, without someone to lean against in the night, there is no freedom from the lonely dog barks in the back of your brain.

I rested after I ate, then drove back to Richie Conway's. He was still gone. I didn't want to walk Bishop's lonely streets nor sit in a bar all night. There was nothing in Bishop for me now.

I drove ninety-four miles back to Bridgeport. There was plenty to do there tomorrow.

Chapter 7

I spent the night in Bridgeport camped beside the road, occasionally waking to the roar of diesels and the whisking of summer vacationers as their motors rushed, then faded into the distance. Up early, grabbed some milk and donuts at a market, and as soon as the courthouse opened, I was back in the vault, going over Mono County files, thinking I might have overlooked Rosa May the first time through. I also searched for records regarding Emma Goldsmith, supposedly the other Bodie madam. I did not find a single reference for either woman.

I was about to drive to Carson City when I thought of early Bodie newspapers. Asking around the courthouse, I was told that Slick Bryant, who ran the motel across the way, had a collection of Bodie newspapers.

The Bryants were one of the earliest pioneer families to settle in Bridgeport. In 1863, Amasa Foster Bryant was drawn to the area by the Aurora boom, a mining camp seventeen miles north of Bodie. Finding Aurora congested with businesses, he settled in Bridgeport and set up a general merchandise store. In 1877 he succombed to Bodie's golden beckon and had a large store there, but returned to Bridgeport in 1881 when Bodie's mines declined.

His son, Amasa S. Bryant, also did his share of history making. A man of faith and vision, he believed in the telephone and brought its service to Bridgeport. His small telephone company ran lines and service out to Bodie and north to Fales Hot Springs.

Slick Bryant, son of Amasa S., was born in 1899, and but for a brief period, lived his entire life in Bridgeport. Since the area was so sparsely settled, Slick knew most everybody in the area. This was helpful in locating families that had once lived in Bodie.

Because of Slick's deep interest in preserving the local history, he was a big help, often introducing me to families soothing an otherwise awkward interview with a stranger. One woman Slick introduced me to, for years had held the key to Rosa's story.

During the warm summer months, Slick and his hard working wife, Marceline, ran Slick's Court. The wings of the motel made a horseshoe shape in the center of which were several shade trees. Underneath the trees were several tables and chairs surrounded by rose bushes and other flowering plants. After deer season, Slick and Marceline closed the motel for the winter months, retiring to their home behind the motel.

Slick Bryant sat in his green golf cart watering the lawn as I walked up. The old man clutched the nozzle with both hands with difficulty. Several of his fingers were missing from each hand. Slick was wearing a T-shirt, his thin grey hair was brushed back and gold wire rim glasses sat wisely on his thin nose. A days growth of stubble had sprouted on his face and neck, and you couldn't help but notice that Slick's legs were gone from just above the knee.

I recall one evening. Slick and I were going through several photo albums. He grinned broadly when we came to this one picture of him taken twenty years ago. Slick was standing on his long legs, holding a giant fish up with both hands, grinning like a fool, his hair still thick and dark. Looking at Slick, I could see he was proud of the great fish, and I think proud, too, for me to see him as he once was.

But the years had come and Slick's legs had gone and somehow his body had grown smaller the way an old man's body does. I never asked Slick about his legs. Someone mentioned Slick's circulation had become so poor, in order to live Slick's legs had to be amputated. During our several meetings together, I never heard Slick complain of his loss or mention it. I admired his courage. He was always joking, always witty, always glad to see you and help you if he could. Whenever I visited him, there was always someone there to talk with hm, he had many friends. Slick was able to make people feel comfortable with his own great loss, never causing people to pity him. It seemed everybody in Bridgeport knew Slick, he was well liked and respected. At this writing, Slick's been dead about four months.

Slick Bryant did have a large collection of Bodie papers which he had rescued from someone's trash heap. Aware of their historical value, he had bundled them up and brought them home. The papers were now in the vault of the Assessor's office. Slick's son, Dan Bryant, kept them there for protection. Dan had the early papers photographed and they were now on microfilm. (The newspapers were from the Bodie Miner Index, 1881-83.) I was free to look at the papers if I wished.

But there would be no point in it really. Being crippled like he was, Slick had plenty of time to read and reread the Bodie papers. He assured me that he had never come across Rosa May. I was disappointed but that was that.

But the interviews I had with Slick, and the picture he painted of the Bodie he knew seventy years ago, was worth as much as anything I might have learned through the old Bodie newspapers.

Born so late in the last century, Slick never knew Rosa May but he remembered Ernest Marks and Billy Owens. In those days they referred to Marks' bar as Marks' Saloon. Like others, Slick remembered that Marks was crippled and walked with a cane. He couldn't remember much else about him.

Billy Owens was the Bodie Justice of the Peace and the town's undertaker. Slick remembered Billy as a small fella, well liked.

Outside of Ella Cain's story, he had never heard of Marks and Owens fighting over Rosa. Nor did he recall ever hearing of the pneumonia epidemic that killed Rosa. He assured me, pneumonia, as well as several other diseases, claimed many lives in the early days. I kept asking Slick about Marks and Rosa, hoping I might shake something loose in his memory, but he remembered nothing more than I've said.

Slick was raised in Brigeport but often visited Bodie with his father, becoming friends with many of the camp's families. The first time he went to Bodie was about 1908, Slick was nine. His first memory of Bodie was watching forty or fifty burros meandering down the road, each loaded with a quarter cord of wood. Their Chinese keepers had harvested pinon pines from the hills outside Bodie. They sold the wood to the townspeople, but their largest customer was the Standard Mill which consumed twenty to thirty cords a day. The Standard would later convert to electrical energy causing many Chinamen to lose their means of living, forcing them to move elsewhere. These Chinamen woodcutters lived in wood camps several miles from Bodie and in the Chinatown area at the north end of town, west of Main Street. The houses of prostitution were in Chinatown which Bodie was never without.

The Standard was a twenty-stamp mill. Its job was to pulverize gold ore which would later be amalgamated with mercury. Compared to Viriginia City's Consolidated Mill, which had eighty stamps; Bodie's Standard was a baby. Yet Slick vividly remembered how the pounding of one stamp vibrated the entire town and the roar of the mill sounded like cannon fire. The Standard Mill ran continually. The townspeople were sure to awaken if its pounding ever ceased during the night. For the Standard was the heart of their little community. When the Standard did not work, the men did not work, and there would be nothing to pay the grocer, the butcher or the shoe clerk. Bodie was completely dependent on its mines. The town eventually folded because the milling of low grade ore did not create a substantial profit.

Bodie's Main Street stretched north and south. To the east was Bodie Bluff, and running south from the bluff was Silver Hill where other mines were located. Both sides of Main Street had the usual wooden buildings with high false fronts, all freshly painted bright white. East and west of Main were the many cottages where the miners and their families lived. Their houses were quite small and without insulation. They were heated by wood burning stoves and light was provided by kerosene lamps. A tank was attached to the kitchen stove where water was heated for bathing. Water was also piped into the kitchen sink. Outhouses were as much a part of life as milk and butter. Some of the miner's cottages and various businesses had electricity after 1912, brought into Bodie by long distance transmission from Green Creek, about fifteen miles away.

In 1908, Slick figured Bodie must have had a population of about a thousand, served by several businesses. (This estimation is quite high. Emil Billeb, author of **Mining Camp Days,** arriving in Bodie in 1908 as a young man, estimated that there were no more than three hundred people.)

There were quite a number of saloons, Slick remembered three: Marks', Maestretti's and Seiler's. There was a brewery, naturally run by an Irishman, John McKenzie. McKenzie's saloon faced Main Street and the brewery was directly behind the saloon. McKenzie's beer is supposed to have been very good, going for 5¢ a pony schooner, a small mug of beer.

During winter, the saloon keepers harvested ice from a reservoir on top of Bodie Bluff. They stored the ice underground in sawdust for use in summer.

There were several general merchandise stores: Cecil Burkham's, Bill Reading's, Harvey Boone's and Tom Moyle's. Two butcher shops, one run by Clarence Wedertz, and the City Market, with meat carvers Donnely and Eli Johl, who married Lottie, the red light girl.

There were two hotels: the Occidental and the U.S. and several boarding houses. The hotels provided a bar and reasonable meals. Many bachelor miners lived in the boarding houses.

Men and women wore hats. A hat for a man was an absolute must and he wouldn't be caught without one. Women, of course, wore long dresses and had their hair pinned up neatly.

During Bodie's long winters, dances were held at the Miner's Union Hall. Slick's band often played at these. Bodie was without a library or the customary opera house. Families most often entertained friends at home.

In summer, Booker Flat, a large field on the south edge of town, was often used for picnics and baseball games. The Bodie baseball team played teams from Tonopah, Hawthorne,

Bridgeport and other nearby towns. These teams took turns traveling by horse and wagon the many miles between their towns for the pleasure of heated competition.

The Bodie Slick knew as a kid, was a small town. There was one school for all grades and two churches, the Methodist and the Catholic. Many families were large and worked hard to subsist on the $4 a day miners made risking their lives in dangerous shafts. With the town so small, everyone knew each other and often helped each other in times of need. By today's standards, Bodie's people would seem poor, but for the time, the small shantys teeming with children was quite common.

The interview with Slick took up the morning and part of the afternoon. Afterward, I walked over to Stuart and Sadie Cain's, Slick's neighbors. Sadie and Stuart were born in Bodie in 1891 and were raised in the camp. Stuart is the son of Jim Cain, Bodie banker and mining man. Because Stuart and Sadie were older and grew up in Bodie, Slick thought they might be of more help.

Stuart Cain met me at the door. At eighty-four, he had a remarkably boyish face with hazy blue eyes. I introduced myself and explained what I was doing.

Stuart smiled when I mentioned Rosa May but he offered nothing. I had been warned Stuart could be talkative about his home town or quite reticent. Today Stuart was reticent. At another time, I would speak with Sadie, who had a marvelous memory and was willing to talk. She is one of few who saw Rosa May alive.

I walked back to Slick's and explained what had happened. He smiled. I thanked him for his help and said I'd write him when I got back south. He wished me luck, we shook hands and I pushed my aging VW further down the road.

I headed out of Bridgeport on 182, went through some mountains, then down into the hot desert again. Near Lucky Boy pass, I caught highway 22 and went north toward Yerington, Nevada. Markham Trailkill and Mrs. Bell lived in Yerington and I had been told that both could provide information on early Bodie and Rosa May.

Yerington is in Smith Valley. Like Bridgeport, the Walker River runs through the valley making it green with plenty of good grazing for sheep and cattle ranchers. Yerington itself is a small town, but a metropolis compared to Bridgeport.

I found Markham Trailkill's address easily. It was a large, rambling two story boarding house for old folks. I climbed the stairs, then walked down a dark musty hall and knocked on Trailkill's door. He wasn't in. I walked back to the lobby and asked around for Trailkill. An elderly friend said I'd find him at a bar and casino on Main Street.

Markham Trailkill was sitting at an empty blackjack table. His newspaper was spread across the green felt. He was a grey headed fella in his seventies and he wore glasses. He was friendly and over beers we talked about Bodie and Rosa May.

Markham Trailkill told me the strangest story I ever heard about Rosa May and one I've never heard since. Yes, he said, Rosa May was buried in the outcast cemetery. She had died as Ella Cain had said, during what Trailkill called a "black pneumonia" epidemic. Black pneumonia killed within twenty-four hours. A miner could be sitting beside you one day and be dead the next. Trailkill believed Rosa died while helping miners and that she was buried outside the fence. However; according to Trailkill, in time people saw their error and repented. They went back to the cemetery, dug Rosa up and buried her again— this time in the regular cemetery! Markham Trailkill told me this with a straight face and in all sincerity. I smiled, it was a hard tale to swallow. Trailkill never knew Rosa May. He was born and raised in Yerington and worked one winter out in Bodie. Because of his more distant relationship with the camp, I doubted his story very much.

I left Yerington and drove out of town to the ranch where Mrs. Bell lived. Just before the ranch, I made my way through a throng of cattle being herded down a country road.

Mrs. Bell, then in her mid-nineties, lived in a mobile home on her son-in-law's ranch. She was the oldest woman I'd yet interviewed, silver haired, thin, dark wrinkled skin, cloudy eyes; and because of her senility, very difficult to communicate with.

I spoke with Mrs. Bell for an hour about Bodie and Rosa May. She frequently apologized for her memory which was failing her this day. At this time, I believed Mrs. Bell was perhaps my last chance to learn something substantial about Rosa's life through old-timers. Mrs. Bell was born during Bodie's boom. I thought I could not possibly find anyone older.

Between her failing memory and her fading in and out of our conversation, Mrs. Bell provided a few gems.

In her clear moments, she remembered Marks. She called him the Old Jew. He ran a saloon on the east side of Main, a block south of Jim Cain's bank. He also lived in a little cottage near the Bells, east of Main, behind the row of businesses. He was an old man now and children often chased him and gave him trouble. Mrs. Bell remembered Rosa May and recalled that Marks was good to her and brought her gifts. He had helped her out, the old woman said.

She remembered seeing Rosa May a few times but "good women" never had anything to do with such girls. Prostitutes kept to themselves and lived in the north end in Chinatown. This was all Mrs. Bell could remember. She apologized and faded away for good.

I regret that I did not have a chance to speak again with Mrs. Bell. On a good day I think she might have remembered more. Unfortunately, the old woman died shortly after my visit.

As I left Mrs. Bell's, the clouds above Smith Valley had gathered and grown somber. They poured torrents on the roads as I drove away. I listened to the splashing of my wheels as I left Yerington and headed toward Carson City.

The interview with Mrs. Bell had disheartened me. I felt I had come so close to learning something substantial about Rosa's life, but I had missed it. Now the hope of learning anything further from old-timers was beginning to fade. I was tired, too, from five frantic days on the road driving all over hell asking strangers questions. I wished I had started this search several years earlier before many of the old-timers had died. I would have had better luck. I felt every fiber in me straining to reach Rosa's life through seven decades. I wondered if I was wasting my time in this bazaar search. I could once again feel the presence of someone with me there in the car. What did it want? I was doing the best I could and I was tired. This was crazy. Perhaps, this someone, had something special to offer me and I would find it if I looked hard enough. I would see.

I planned to make Carson City by evening but I was tired and discouraged and sick of driving. I stopped in Gardnerville, twenty miles south. I had promised myself that I would not spend my money foolishly on motels, but I succombed to an aching desire for a hot shower and a good night's sleep. It was worth the eighteen dollars. I slept until eleven the next morning.

I planned to check public records in Carson City and Virginia City for information regarding Rosa, Marks and Emma Goldsmith. According to Ella Cain, Rosa had worked in brothels in both towns. I was guessing, but I figured Emma Goldsmith also came from this area before moving on to Bodie. I was hoping to find evidence that Rosa and Emma had owned houses of prosititution in Carson and Virginia City. I knew my chances were slim. Prostitutes seldom owned property and very often madams themselves did not own their houses. From the envelopes addressed to Rosa May in the Bodie Museum and from Ella Cain's story, I knew that Rosa had lived at No. 1 Ormsby Street, Carson City and at 18 South D Street, Virginia City. If Rosa had not owned houses at these addresses, I hoped to learn who had.

Before searching Carson City records, I drove up and down Ormsby Street, now called Curry, admiring the huge cottonwoods that shaded the broiling street. It was along Ormsby Street that the red light had extended for several blocks. I was looking for what might have been No. 1 Ormsby Street. I remembered that Frank Balfe said the remaining houses of prostitution were torn down several years ago.

I later learned that No. 1 Ormsby Street would have been at the corner of King and Ormsby Streets. There were several reasons why this would have been a good location for a brothel. For one, the Nevada State Legislature met only a block away on Carson Street, the main thoroughfare, along which were many businesses and hotels. Secondly, the Virginia and Truckee Railroad depot was only seven blocks north at Caroline and Carson Streets. The United States Mint at Carson was right across from the train depot.

A brothel at King and Ormsby streets, then, was in the middle of the business district through which many men moved. Nevada legislators, train travelers, mint workers and men who worked at the Empire mills, several miles away, were likely customers.

I spent the morning and part of the afternoon in the Carson Courthouse searching land and death records for traces of Rosa, Emma Goldsmith and Ernest Marks. As with Mono County records, names were not alphabetized which made an easy job tedious.

I searched records from 1868 to 1901 and did not find a thing. I was disappointed but that was that.

I drove up Carson Street crowded with summer travelers. I bought ice and food at a Safeway market and parked in the shade. There I eagerly devoured cold, sweet and sour plums and nectarines. My eyes were tired from searching faded records for several hours. After six days and nights on the road alone, research had wearied me. I had learned a few things more about Rosa, but not as much as I had hoped. I had no idea then, that it would take another three years to finish the task I had started. All I knew was that I was tired, terribly hot and hungry. I would go through Virginia City records and feeling somewhat discouraged, drive the five hundred miles back to Riverside.

From Carson City you go northeast on highway 50 until the two lane highway becomes four lanes and climbs the hills. About ten miles from Carson a sign points north and you drive another eleven miles to Gold Hill and Virginia City.

The land out here is fiercely dry and barren, covered by the ever present white sagebrush. There are no trees. Because of the terrible heat, the land is far more inhospitable than the cooler mountains where Bodie lies.

The road to Virginia City winds through what is known as Gold Canyon, where gold and silver were discovered in 1859 causing the mining camps of Gold Hill and Virginia City to sprout up. The two mining camps, a mile apart but working the same Comstock Lode, prospered for twenty years, the most profitable period 1873-79, the boom years. In 1879 when Bodie boomed, Virginia City began losing her population of twenty thousand. As with the death of all mining camps, the lack of rich ore drove the money hungry souls elsewhere. It has been said that there never was a mining camp as grand as Virginia City and never will be one like it again. Virginia City's mines poured out hundreds of millions of dollars which helped the Union win the Civil War and established San Francisco as a major city.

As you drive up Gold Canyon, you read the tourist signs, all freshly painted with bright summer colors. The signs tell of Virginia City's past glory, of her most well known citizen, Mark Twain; and of the various saloons, mine tunnels and famous houses one can visit. Up the steep canyon, you pass a small cluster of houses, huge caverns and piles of golden sand. This is Gold Hill. A hundred years earlier Gold Hill had five to seven thousand citizens, throngs of bars, hundreds of buildings and a newspaper. They are all gone.

A mile beyond Gold Hill the canyon becomes steeper, you reach a switch-back, the car lugs, finally you reach the crest — the Divide, where Mark Twain was robbed, then down and your on C Street, Virginia City's main thoroughfare.

Virginia City is built on the side of a barren mountain, once called Sun Mountain but known today as Mount Davidson. Streets running horizontally across the mountain are lettered, the highest being A Street. The poorest people lived farther down the mountain nearer to the mines and the horrible noise from the mills.

The mines are scattered about the mountain, the most profitable are located below D Street. The huge piles of earth and stone the miners took out of the mines so long ago are still here for the tourist to marvel at. But the hoisting works, the stamp mills, the smoke stacks and mine buildings that once covered this area are gone and the area seems strangely deserted. The mining companies salvaged their equipment when they were done with Virginia City.

The Virginia City red light was on D Street and ran for several blocks near the train depot. It was at 18 South D Street that Rosa once lived. I looked for the address but was disappointed to find all but one of the cribs gone. A mere bronze marker told of the district's active days.

I spent the afternoon in the Virginia City courthouse searching the heavy indexes for traces of Rosa, Ernest Marks, and Emma Goldsmith. Because of Virginia City's greater success there were more indexes and more names, none alphabetized. I didn't finish my work until the clerk was ready to shut her doors. Several hours of searching had proved utterly fruitless. I was ready to go home.

Discouraged and tired but not defeated. On my way back to Riverside I interviewed three more old-timers and luck was with me.

In Lee Vining, I spoke with Mrs. Katie Bell who had lived in Bodie. Mrs. Bell was in her seventies.

Katie Bell never knew Rosa May but she had heard about her. She claimed Rosa May was a good hearted woman who helped the poor and low whenever she could. That was all Katie could say but she believed her brother, Richie Conway in Bishop, would certainly know more. In Bishop there was also Anna McKenzie who had lived in Bodie. Anna might know something more.

I zipped down to Bishop and this time Richie Conway was home. He was a ruddy faced old man, very warm and friendly.

Richie Conway explained, very simply, that he had seen Rosa May when he was about seven years old. Born in 1895, this would make the time around 1902. Richie had delivered milk to her in the red light many times. He remembered her as a dark haired, middle aged woman. She was a big hearted woman, he said, and never let anyone go hungry. Richie believed that she had had a large funeral.

Richie remembered the times as a kid that his dad took him into the saloons where the red light girls were. The girls would pick little Richie up, set him on the bar and say, "Give him a drink, give him a drink."

That was all Richie could remember. He wished he could have told me more but he wasn't about to invent any tall tales. I believed him.

Finally, as I was about to give up hope that anyone alive had seen Rosa May, Richie Conway claimed he had seen her in 1902. I was elated and very surprised that Rosa had lived so late. Pleased with my minor success, I rushed over to Anna McKenzie for my last interview.

Anna McKenzie was born in Bodie in 1896. Her grandmother ran a two story brick boarding house in Bodie next to the Odd Fellows Hall. Anna's husband, Mervin McKenzie; dead several years, was a cousin of Bill Glenn's, the first old-timer I interviewed by letter.

Anna wished Mervin was alive. She said that he could have told me more about the Bodie red light and Rosa May. After all, it was men who knew about those things.

Anna remembered that the Bodie prostitutes seldom came uptown. Instead; they phoned for groceries, ice and beer to be delivered. Anna's husband, Mervin, delivered groceries to "those women." The red light girls kept to themselves and were well ordered. Anna recalled that they seemed kind hearted. When a miner died, it was common custom among the prostitutes to take up a collection and offer the money anonymously to the miner's family.

Anna saw Rosa May once. Anna was twelve or fourteen, making the year about 1908-10. She thought that Rosa was a quiet woman who kept to herself.

As a child, she also remembered seeing Lottie Johl, an

ex-prostitute. After Lottie died Anna heard that Jim Cain bought Lottie's house.

In 1916, Bodie was slowing down. John McKenzie sold his brewery and saloon and left town. The red light girls were all gone by 1917 and it seemed to Anna that Rosa May must have died before this. She could not recall Rosa's death nor news of her funeral.

In parting, Anna offered the name of Guy McInnis, a man in his mid-nineties who was a bookkeeper for Cecil Burkham. Burkham had owned a dry goods store and operated a stage between Bodie and Hawthorne. Anna believed Mr. McInnis to be the oldest survivor of Bodie. He was nearly blind and lived in Hawthorne.

I was pleased to find two people who had seen Rosa May, and pleased to learn that she had lived as late as 1910. This would make research easier.

True, I had not found an intimate acquaintance of Rosa's, but Richie and Anna were a beginning. I drove home happy.

A month later, I made another trip to the Bridgeport-Bodie area for further interviews. It was my desire to locate the Rosa May letters which had been auctioned off in 1934 when Billy Owens died. You may recall that his property was bought by a certain B.C. Honea.

Through Slick Bryant I learned that a Honea ran a motel in Lee Vining. In Lee Vining I discovered that a Briscoe Charles Honea had died several years earlier. His grandson, also named Briscoe, knew nothing about the Rosa May letters but he showed me the house his grandfather bought at the Bodie auction which was later moved to Lee Vining. He also gave me the address of Chloe Clay, Honea's daughter, who might know something about the letters.

I was to have better luck. When I returned to Bridgeport, Slick Bryant introduced me to Helen Evans, Ella Cain's daughter.

Helen Evans, then in her early seventies, was eager to

help me. Asking if she knew anything about the Rosa May letters, she said, "Oh yes, I have twenty or thirty of them at home in Pasadena."

It was Ella Cain who bought Rosa's trunk at the 1934 auction, the trunk that contained Rosa's clothing, photographs and letters.

Helen Evans summered in Bridgeport with her husband and lived the rest of the year in Pasadena. I would be free to look at Rosa's letters when Helen returned to Pasadena in October or November.

After two months of searching I had finally found documents through which I might learn a great deal about Rosa's life.

BOOK II

Chapter 8

Hollywood. The Rosa May research was temporarily laid aside. I was back in Southern California and ready to begin recording the long awaited album — the Big Dream.

Before the Mammoth gig, Kevin and I had met a group of record producers who owned a 16-track recording studio in Pasadena. They had had one big hit record and they were looking for another. Supposedly, we were one of the acts they hoped could put them back on the charts.

They had listened to a demo (demonstration) tape of thirty of my songs and they felt the material was strong. They wanted Kevin and I to record an album for them. The producers would attempt to sell the album outright to a large label. If things went well, our album would be distributed throughout the country, and with enough air-play bolstering sales, there was a chance I could become a wealthy young songwriter.

Unfortunately, things didn't turn out as we had hoped they would.

In time, the producers offered us a Producer/Artist Contract, fourteen pages of legalistic mumbo-jumbo. With the aid of Webster's dictionary and several hours of hair pulling, Kevin and I managed to decipher the contract. It was a sham, vague and tricky. It would leave us with a stack of bills that would take us years to pay.

Once we understood the contract, we were depressed. All summer long we had looked forward to recording our album and now we discovered we had nearly been tricked into a very bad situation. It was disappointing. There would be no album, not now, not with these record producers.

By now, I had moved to Pasadena, it seemed the place to live. We were recording our album there and singing three nights at a club. Helen Evans also lived in Pasadena and I was eagerly awaiting her return so I could read the Rosa May letters.

We sang in Pasadena for several months at a posh, new restaurant, where valets swiftly hid customer's cars in the restaurant's vast parking lot. The owner of the restaurant was not especially sensitive to musicians. He hid us in a dark corner of his bar. His customers ripped the hammers out of my piano and spilled drinks on the keys and woodwork. The audiences, if you could call them that, were rich and rude, and the thick cigarette smoke was nauseating.

One bad night it all came to a head. The owner gave us hell about something and I told him to take a walk. He fired us, but I really didn't care. I was sick of bars, booze and reckless living and audiences that didn't give a damn. I wanted to sing my music for people who would listen, who weren't running away from their problems, who were eager to feel— not anesthetize their feelings with alcohol.

True, I was earning a living in bars, but it was a hard life and it was getting me nowhere as a songwriter. It was time to make the rounds with my songs in Hollywood. It would be tough, but the greatest artistic and financial success would come in Hollywood, or so I thought at the time.

I stopped working in bars and decided to earn my living in some healthier way. Soon my savings was gone and I started looking for work.

In order to push my songs in Hollywood during the day, I was going to need a part-time night job. That in itself limited the choice of jobs.

I was stone broke when I finally landed a bartending job at a pizza parlour. I was so hard-up, I lied to get the job. I told the manager I was married and my wife was expecting. A grey haired, middle aged man, he knew about babies and bills and he gave me the job. Now and then he asked about my wife and I had to lie to him again. I didn't like lying but I had needed the job desperately.

So there I was, college graduate, professional musician, struggling songwriter, stumbling historical researcher — pouring beer and soda for $2.20 an hour and grateful to get that. I worked from four to twelve and during the days, hustled my songs in Hollywood, that fabled town of dreams and illusions.

My plan in Hollyood was to interest a publisher. A publisher's job is to locate potential money-making hits. Once a song is signed to a publisher and later recorded, the publisher and songwriter split whatever profits are made.

It is also the publisher's job to get songs to producers or artists or recording company people. It must be made clear here that a producer is someone who gathers songs which he believes will suit a certain artist he is working with. The producer then shows the song to the artist. If the artist feels good about the song and believes it is a potential Hit, he will record the song. The song is recorded on tape and later transferred by a complicated mechanical process to vinyl discs — records. The records are distributed by the artist's record company to radio stations and record stores throughout the country and often the world. If the artist is very lucky, the record company's promotion people get behind the song and really push it. The marketing techniques and promotion of an artist and his record, in many cases determines whether or not a song will become a Hit. If the marketing people do a successful job, the song will get a lot of airplay, and the public will go out and buy the record.

If the record does not become a Hit nor even get on the charts, sales will suffer and no one will make any money. This includes the songwriter who has nervously watched his song go from the publisher, to the producer, to the artist, to the world — and finally into the garbage can, where thousands of records land each week.

Previous to my venture in Hollywood, I had always written songs to express myself. I tried to create memorable melodies combined with sincere lyrics, from the heart, plain and simple. My motivation for songwriting was expression.

In Hollywood, the idealistic, young songwriter confronts what at first seems an impenetrable monster: The Music Business, or more aptly; the Music Industry, as those who are part of it proudly refer. In Hollywood, the young songwriter sadly discovers that songs are not only written to express one's self, but more often than not they are written to earn great sums of money. There is nothing wrong with songs earning men a living. The problem is, the Music Industry has become a multi-billion dollar business and often, good music and fine songwriters are lost in the Industry's pursuit for the Almighty Dollar. If a song does not at first seem commercial; that is, potentially profitable, a song— even if its a good song, may not receive interest by the Industry. There have been many songs rejected by the Industry that have become enormous Hits. **You Light Up My Life,** recorded recently by Debbie Boone, was such a song. Joe Brooks, the songwriter, brought **You Light Up My Life** around to every major music publisher. The song was rejected by each publisher, not once, but several times. It was quite an embarassment when the song went on to become an all time best seller and Joe Brooks received a Grammy for writing it.

Brooks' story is a common one. The rejection of good songs and fine songwriters by publishers and recording companies drives many struggling artists to booze, drugs— and sometimes suicide, and I'm not being over-dramatic. I've been through it and I've seen what the rejection and frustration can do.

Many Hit Songs are very good songs. Many are also pure junk written by desperate songwriters who are sick to death of loneliness and utter frustration, who have fallen victims to the enticings of greedy men, well aware of the banal likes of fourteen year olds and know how to satisfy their adolescent longings with trash.

Most everybody in the Music Industry is looking for a Hit song, whether they are in Hollywood, New york, Nashville, London— whererever. And most everybody has his own ideas of what a Hit song is, for what seems like a Hit to one person may not seem so to another.

On the West Coast, people in the business are aware their livelihood stems from the young songwriters on the street who are eventually discovered and become money-makers. Therefore; some of the publishing houses do allow a guy off the street to make an appointment and come in and show two or three of his **best** songs. But even in Hollywood, the number of publishers with such an open door policy is small. Most often a writer has to send his songs in on a cassette or reel-to-reel tape along with lyrics. Someone at the publishing house is supposed to listen to the tapes. Most everyone sending tapes around gets them back with a polite note: "We appreciate your interest in our company, but I'm afraid we cannot use your material. Feel free to send us your new songs." In essence, you get a big, fat, "NO!" After enough rejection slips you begin to wonder if you're a songwriter after all.

Every Monday, I called the publishing houses and made appointments to see people. I had to call early and I had to call Monday or I wouldn't be seeing anyone that week and a whole week of hustling would be wasted.

When I met with a publisher, I brought my guitar — and my tapes — and sang the songs right in the publisher's office. I felt this was a much more personal approach than just playing one of my tapes. Nearly everyone appreciated this method. I also brought a typed copy of my lyrics, neatly covered in clear plastic so publishers could handle the lyrics and I wouldn't have to re-type them again.

Most of the big Hollywood publishers have their offices in the several high-rise buildings on the 6400 block of West Sunset. You walk into the expansive lobbies of these buildings, find the directory and locate the floor and room of the publisher you have an appointment with.

When you reach the floor, the elevator dumps you into a plushly carpeted hallway. There, you wonder quite nervously what you're doing and whether you're a songwriter after all. This is the first time you've seen a publisher and you're about to have the first professional judgement of your material. And to put it honestly, you're scared to death of the ego destruction this publishing dude is about to heap on you, and rightly so.

75

You walk down one hallway to the left of the elevator only to discover you're on the wrong side of the building. You go back to the elevator, cross over to the next hallway and find Zeke Publishing. You knock, walk in and find yourself in a small reception area with thick carpet, leather couch, various Music Industry magazines on the table, and a pretty receptionist who asks you who you are and what you want. You explain you have an appointment with so and so. She tells you he'll be out shortly. You sit on the couch feeling quite jittery. Mouth dry, you check and re-check to see if you've brought everything. You've got the right tape for the right publisher with the correct order of songs. You've got the right lyric sheets. Your guitar is tuned, you're all set. For twelve years you've been putting words and music together, you know you're good and still your nervous. You don't know why, but yes you do. This guy's going to pronounce judgement on your material in about five minutes, the material which is the basis of your dream, your hope, that precious part of you that doesn't want to get stepped on. You want this guy to go absolutely nuts over your songs and if he doesn't, you're gonna feel crushed.

The door opens, and a long haired young man your age introduces himself. He's dressed in jeans and a T-shirt but he's still a businessman no matter how laid-back he looks. You smile, shake his hand, try to talk confidently; he leads you through a door, down a hall to his office. His office is small, there might be an out of tune piano on one wall, a large desk with tapes and papers and lead sheets scattered across it. He might have a few posters or pictures of artists tacked to the wall, artists he handles the publishing for. He sits down behind his desk. He wants to know about you. How long have you been in Hollywood? Have you ever been published? What's your track record (any Hit songs)? How long have you been writing songs, etc. He eyes you with an objective business-like coldness. He doesn't have time to waste. He asks if you want to play your tapes on his machines on the rack behind his desk. No, you'd rather sing them yourself.

So now it's all yours. You've got to prove to this guy that you're a great songwriter and that your songs will make him and his company a lot of money.

You unlatch the metal snaps on your guitar case, take your guitar out, reach in your pocket for a pick, sit back down. Closing your eyes, you try to make your thoughts go back to that special moment when you first started writing this song. Though the deep feeling that helped to create the song is gone, once you open your mouth and begin to sing, strumming the chords of your song, the melody pours out from all the love in your soul. There it is again, that magic you felt soaring in you as you wrote the song, and chills are going up your back, just like that night, that night very late when the music began singing in you and somehow with God's gift and lots of hard work you were able to bring the song out of your soul and into the world of sound. And now you're not thinking about that guy listening to you or what he thinks, and the jittery feeling's leaving your stomach, replaced with a lovely warmth, the warmth of your love and your belief in your child: your song.

You finish singing, you open your eyes, and your eyes are meeting his, and you see that they've softened considerably and he's got a little smile on his face. Your waiting, you want to know what this professional thinks of your song and now he begins to tell you. You've got talent and he knows you've worked hard, you've got potential. The song is a good song, but it's not a Hit song and he needs Hit songs. But he relaxes now, he knows your not some fool off the street who picked up a guitar six months ago and thinks he's a songwriter. And in his knowing that you've got something, you begin to relax. He wants to hear more, so you sing a couple more songs. He's impressed, you're good, but the songs just aren't Hit songs. He would like to have a tape, so you hand him a cassette with your copyright seal, name and address.

That's all that can happen today. You walk out of his office feeling ambivalent. You're not a failure, you're not a success. You're not in nor out, you're just hanging, and the rent is due tomorrow and you're not a Hit songwriter yet and you're worried.

You have an appointment with another guy an hour later. You hang around the street for that hour and then climb up another building to another publishing representative where the same scene is acted out. And the next day you see someone else, and the next day someone else and they all say the same: you're a good songwriter, you've got good songs, but they're not Hit songs and you try not to believe them.

After a few weeks you've seen quite a number of people, just about all you can get in and see. The news spreads fast among the different publishers that a new writer is in town and he's pretty good but he's not **hot** yet. Someday he might make someone a lot of money. But the publishers just watch him, unwilling to take a chance on his material. In time, one will bite, and then all will want one of his songs. But now the young songwriter is just a small fish in a big pond and they'll wait and see how big he gets. The publishers have got time and a decent income behind them. The young songwriter just has his songs and his hope, but hope is something that can easily wither away. If he's not strong, he may grow bitter, and the songs he once could write easily, won't come at all. Still, he hopes with every appointment that he'll finally meet that someone who will at last **hear** his songs and become aware of his enormous talent. This is the songwriter's dream and it is sometimes realized.

Having met with several publishers, I would drive home to Pasadena. The interviews and being excited all day took a lot out of me. Home, I would grab something to eat and lie down, my mind whirling, wondering if I would ever sign with a publisher, whether I would ever see any of the millions songwriters were making. And through it all, when I got to the end of the road, when I was a success, would I still be the same sensitive person, or would I be just another songwriter Hollywood seduced, another cunning businessman who had long forgotten why he dreamed of becoming a songwriter. And finally, see myself thrown into the Music Industry's garbage bin, where all busted, sold out, songwriters end. Ah yes, this was show business, the glamor and the glory, the striving for the tinsel star.

Those days I was unable to meet with publishers, I spent in part writing and taping new songs; writing the Rosa May novel, which was going terribly—and researching.

At the Pasadena Library, I gathered and read volumes on Bodie and Virginia City, California and Nevada history; and, of course, prostitution. Slowly I was getting a feel for Rosa's era, and how prostitutes fit into the scheme of early California and Nevada life.

I also spent many hours at the Los Angeles Museum of Natural History. There I searched and found early photos of Bodie and Virginia City. I also checked early City Directories and Pacific Coast Directories for Rosa May, hoping to get a rough idea of where she was during what years.

John Cahoon, L.A. Museum curator, was particularly helpful. He turned me on to A.A. Forbes, a Bishop photographer who visited Bodie in the late 1890's up until 1910 or so. During his summer stays, Forbes shot a hoard. of Bodie photographs, one of which is included in the photo section. The photo is an excellent shot showing the Bodie red light and Rosa May's house.

In addition, John Cahoon informed me of the Burton Frasher photograph collection at the Pomona Library. Burton Frasher accompanied Carl Parcher Russell, a writer, to Bodie in the fall of 1927. It was Frasher's 1927 photos of the Bodie cemetery that eventually led me to the discovery of Rosa May's actual gravesite. (Photo section.)

I still had not located documents regarding Rosa's death. In efforts to do so, I contacted the Methodist and Catholic churches, the only churches that had established themselves in Bodie. The searching of their records took many months. The search for a death record by archivists proved fruitless. Later, I made efforts to locate families of priests and ministers who had served in Bodie, hoping a journal or a log might have been passed down which would mention Rosa May's death. This, was also, a dead end.

However; my correspondence with the Methodist Church put me in contact with Will Ralph, Methodist Archivist at Berkely.

Will Ralph had visited Bodie in 1961, at which time he took a picture of Rosa's grave. (Photo section.) The wooden post and sign marked Rosa's gravesite previous to Louis Serventi's marker.

It was in the L.A. Museum library that I came across Carl Parcher Russell's article, **"The Bodie That Was,"** which appeared in the November, 1929 issue of Touring Topics (now Westways). Included in the article were some of Burton Frasher's photos.

It was during his visit to Bodie for the article, that Russel met Earnest Marks and interviewed him. In the following excerpt, Russell calls Marks, "Smith," and refers to Rosa May as, "Rosemary." Speaking of Maiden Lane, the Bodie red light, Russell explains the relationship between Rosa May and Ernest Marks:

Here "Rosemary" reigned for a time and with one, whom we shall call Smith, maintained a noted business of prostitution and gambling.

Their partnership was quite as successful as some of the mining combinations on the mountainside above their den. Wealth flowed into their household, and Rosemary sported huge jewels and rich raiment. But Rosemary died. We may believe that the dapper Smith grieved, but he was not overcome. He took unto himself another mistress. Partner number two fell short of Rosemary in business ability and sincerity toward Smith. At an opportune time she absconded and with her went a goodly share of the cash assets of the business, as well as the best jewels and furs left by the late Rosemary. A manager of the proper philosophic attitude was essential to the Maiden Lane branch of the business and Smith accepted a third partner. Like her predecessor, she laid hands upon more than a paltry of the accumulated wealth, and the cream of the remaining Rosemary jewels. How many times this drama of chance-taking and loss was enacted only Smith can tell. He is not apt to be found in a reminiscent mood so far as these bits of personal history are concerned. I met him at the door of a dilapidated liquor house on Main Street, and almost at once he displayed to me what I presume is his last jewels of those days of half a century ago. Within the old saloon he frys his bacon and makes his bed, where once milled hundreds of miner's feet. I discovered that his roulette wheel abides with him still.

Absolutely alone on the street of deserted business establishments, he impressed me as a most pathetic individual. Slumped down as he was in an old saloon chair, his withered little form seemed to need more than the feeble autumn sunshine that fell upon it. As I talked to him, his slender, agile fingers played about his vest pockets, and presently he drew forth a gold match case. "That's Bodie ore! Look at it. More gold than quartz. And there is more of it in the old hill yonder. I'll stay till she booms again." One wall of this watch case was formed by a beautifully polished section of very rich quartz. The natural design made by the gold veins imprisoned within the quartz formed an "R."

So here was Ernest Marks, nearly fifty years after Bodie's boom had drawn him, utterly alone, unwilling to speak of his earlier years with Rosa. As Russell and Marks talked, neither knew that Marks would soon join Rosa on the sage covered slopes beyond the town.

Though it was forty-seven years since Russell's article was published, I tried to locate him. Russell was dead and he had not left behind notes of his 1927 interview with Marks.

Chapter 9

Helen Evans returned to Pasadena in mid-November. The morning of our meeting, my VW finally gave up the ghost. I borrowed Kevin's car and made the meeting on time. I brought my notebook and a cassette recorder, Mrs. Evans did not want the letters to leave the house. I would have to read the letters aloud and tape them on the cassette. Later, I would transcribe the letters from tape.

Cordial and silver haired Helen Evans met me at the door and led me to her living room where we spoke briefly. She had set up a card table in the middle of the living room on top of which was a packet of letters. Understanding my eagerness, Helen left me and busied herself with the maid in the kitchen.

I opened the packet of letters and thumbed through them. There seemed to be about thirty letters. Touching them, I felt a strange anxiety, knowing, in a moment, I would be reading letters that were written a hundred years ago and meant to be read only by Rosa May.

I spread the envelopes out on the table. Each letter was still enclosed in its envelope. The envelopes were of various colors: yellow, white, orange and baby blue. All bore the Wells Fargo and Co. insignia. Most of the envelopes were the green, three cent stamped envelopes I first saw at he Bodie Museum. These envelopes, like those at the Museum, had been neatly opened with a knife at the narrow, right end.

As I took the letters from their envelopes, I noticed how the paper was still white and crisp, as it must have looked the day it was written on. I figured the paper had not aged because it had been kept in envelopes, away from air and sun all those years. The rich black ink stood out clearly as the lines of the letters twisted fat and thin from the quill pens used long ago. The ornate writing was difficult to make out in places. Certain letters looked foreign and oddly shaped compared to today's handwriting.

It took three hours to read through all the letters. I read each letter silently, struggling to make out the more obscure words. When I was certain I knew what most of the letter said, I read the letter aloud and taped it on the cassette recorder. I made certain to mention the date it was written, in what city; and, by whom. When I returned to my apartment, I began transcribing the letters from the tape, which took several days.

The packet consisted of twenty-five letters written by eight people over a three and a half year period between September 27, 1876 and March 27, 1880. Most of the letters were addressed to Rosa in Carson and Virginia City. None were addressed to her in Bodie.

Of the twenty-five letters, four are addressed to Rosa in Virginia City. These include the earliest letter, September 27, 1876, and the latest, March 27, 1880. Three of these letters are addressed to Rosa at 18 South D Street, a brothel operated by Cad Thompson, a woman who ran various houses of prostitution on South and North D Street from the 1860's up until the early 1890's.

The Virginia City red light extended along D Street, bounded on the south by Taylor Street, and on the north by Mill Street. Union Street was the dividing line for addresses running north and south. Addresses north of Union, North D Street.

Cad Thompson's brothel at 18 South D Street was on the west side of D, between Union and Taylor. Oddly enough, the City Hall was located in the same block. The Virginia and Truckee passenger depot was near Thompson's place, on the northeast corner of Union and D Street.

Eighteen letters over a one year period, from July 7, 1878 to August 15, 1879, were received by Rosa at various addresses in Carson City. Most of these letters were written by Ernest Marks, Rosa's lover, living at that time in Gold Hill. Rosa had various post office boxes in Carson City: numbers 2, 40 and 49. She also received letters at No. 1 Ormsby Street and in care of Jennie

Moore, a black woman, age 54, who ran a house of prostitution on the northwest corner of Third and Ormsby.

The Carson red light was on Ormsby Street, now called Curry. According to the June 9, 1875 issue of the Carson Appeal, the red light was restricted to Ormsby Street between Second and Fifth streets. Knowing, however; that Rosa received letters at No. 1 Ormsby, which would have been at the corner of King and Ormsby, one block north of fifth, it would seem that the red light ran from Second Street north along Ormsby as far as King Street. This made the Carson red light four blocks long, as large as the Virginia City red light district.

Included in the packet, is one letter Rosa May wrote which was later returned to her. This letter proved invaluable when the letters were examined by handwriting analysts.

And finally, there is one pencil written note by Isaac Isaacs, a Virginia City clothing merchant who asked Rosa to meet him at his room after work, for, shall we say; a private entertainment.

I found my first readings of the letters difficult because I did not know many common expressions of the era, nor did I know who the various people were mentioned in the letters, a total of thirty-six. Through use of City Directories of the period, census and newspapers, I was able to identify most of the thirty-six.

For your convenience and better understanding, as each letter is presented, I will explain common expressions of the era and identify people mentioned. This will make your first reading far more informative than mine.

I know of no other collection of letters written to a Western mining camp prostitute. I have decided to publish all twenty-five letters considering their historical value. I have placed the letters in chronological order and have kept the original spelling and punctuation, as I believe this will reveal the writer's character, his casualness or lack of attentiveness. However; in some letters, I have created paragraphs for easier reading.

The first letter is from Laura Davenport and is addressed to Rosa at 32 South D Street, Virginia City, Nevada:

Wendnesday Afternoon
New York, Sept. 27th, 1876

My Dear Friend Rose,

I received your kind letter and was glad to hear from you once more and also that you have recovered from your chills and fever. I have heard before about that medicine being good and told Joe of it, but he is all go on quinnie [I believe she means quinine] I tell him I guess it makes him feel good. I hope it doese.

Rose I was to a wedding last night at the St. Stephens Church. The couple were real nice looking and the Bride was dress very neat and pretty. The organ played the Wedding March when they were coming in and it sounded beautiful, the Bride's father brought her up to the altar and gave her away. This is the first time since I have been in New York that I ever seen a wedding or rather seen a couple married it tis a kind of solemn thing after all. I was a wishing that I was a good virtuous girl and it was Joe and me but no such good luck, but you can bet if I had my life to live over and knew as much as I do now, I would never do wrong. Well there is no use to look at the past, for that is gone long ago.

I met one of the old sewing women [prostitute] the other day and she told me that Maggie Belmont was a coming on here after women it is time for the Landladies [madams] to make their appearnace from the South and all round. I don't know them girls you mention in your letter. I am glad that your are doing well, try and save some money and come back to New York and I want you to hold my baby and see it. I think Rosa after all these years I am caught [pregnant] I am not fooling I haven't been unwell [had a period] in two months, unless this month shows something and it tis most out now. I feel awfully worried about it, it may come out all right, I hope so.

You want to know if we have joined the church, not exactly. Rose do you ever hear what has become of Sopky

Post. I would really like to know. What is your Landlady name [she could mean, what is your prostitute alias, but more likely, what is your madam's name.] I never of seen it in many a long day, God knows what has become of him, for I don't. Why don't you write to his last address. What was his last name I never knew. Rose just as soon as I get my new Black Silk Suit I am going to send you a good picture of me you might let me have that one I had taken in Havana for I haven't got any that was taken so long ago of me and if anything should happen to you it would only fall into strangers hands. You might let me have it. Well I haven't any more to write this time, the people that I board with is trying to sell out, so I can't tell what minute I shall have to change quarters so you had better direct to the Station.

Good By a kiss Love From Your Friend
Mrs. Laura Davenport

Station Y Third Avenue
Ans. soon
Joe wished to be remembered to you
Excuse poor writing

From this letter it appears that Rosa has been in Virginia City for some time. From Laura's inquiries concerning Sopky Post, we know that Laura and Joe spent time in Virginia City before their recent return to New York. Rosa may have at one time lived in New York, considering Laura's urging that she "try and save some money and come back to New York." This hint, that Rosa came from the east, instead of Paris as Ella Cain said; will be proved with later evidence.

Though Rosa is doing well financially, she has suffered from chills and fever. We do not know what has brought the chills and fever on. By September, Virginia City's nights were growing cold high in the mountains. The red light cribs were flimsy frame shacks which permitted wind and cold to easily enter. Most cribs were small one story buildings with a front and back room. The front room had a few chairs, perhaps a carpet, bureau, mirror and various pictures on the walls, photos of loved ones. The back room consisted of a three-quarter size bed and a pot belly stove fed by wood or coal and used for cooking and heat. There was an outhouse behind the crib.

The flimsy cribs may have partly been the cause of Rosa's chills and fever. However; we know today that illness is not only caused by bacteria and viruses but is also caused by various insecurities we face. The man who worries has backaches. The anxious girl develops ulcers. One wonders whether or not Rosa's chills and fever were caused by the isolation and precariousness of her work and life. For Rosa's illnesses are mentioned by several writers in various letters.

The most interesting and touching part of Laura's letter is the wedding she witnessed. Laura whistfully remarks that a wedding, "is a kind of solemn thing after all," something she wished Joe and her had. She regrets her many years as a prostitute and wishes she was a "good virtuous girl," but such possibilities are "gone long ago." Her father will never be giving her away.

Laura is afraid that she is "caught," pregnant. Pregnancy greatly complicated the prostitute's life. It caused her to lose her means of living for a time which caused troubles with her pimp. Such men even resented a woman's period, as a girl could not work. For Laura, pregnancy meant another responsibility which she would have had great difficulty with.

Since this is the only letter we have of Laura's, we are left to wonder many things. Certainly, the details here do not point toward a happy ending for all concerned.

The photograph mentioned here of Laura in her black silk suit, is very likely the photograph supposedly of Rosa May now at the Bodie Museum. The woman in the photograph only resembles Rosa May, and she is wearing a black silk dress.

Interesting that Rosa asks if Laura and Joe have become members of the church. Many prostitutes were religious. Mexican prostitutes often had crucifixes nailed to their crib walls.

The following letter was written in San Francisco, December 12, 1876, by a man we will simply know as Jack.

My Own Darling Rose —
    I presume you think I do not care much for you by allowing your kind note to remain so long unanswered it is nothing but neglect Rose I have thought of it several times but not having a right good show to ans. let it go until thinking you might become disgusted. I take this show to drop you a line — I see in your last [letter] your natural distrust of me shows up — I tell you darling that if stocks go up I **would** see my little one if only for a short time. You may think it in your minds eye or not — Won't you let me tell the truth once Rose? I think sometimes you mean what you say and its but fast for you to reciprocate — Speaking of that cane my dear as long as you keep it for yourself it will not hurt you — Again if stocks do ever go up I'll make it something better than a cane for you to remember me by. What is the matter with Ophir [a large producing mine in Virginia City] up there. They have knocked the d— h— out if it here — I hope business is good with your darling and that you are happy. If you'll believe me I'll think the world of little Rose

yours,
Jack

This short letter gives us our first clues of Rosa's character. Jack, more than likely, was a customer of Rosa's while he was in Virginia City. There is a hint here that he may have been more to Rosa than a customer, by Jack's referring to Rosa as, "My Own Darling Rose." Whatever terms they were on, it appears that Jack owes Rosa money. Prostitutes during this time, sometimes allowed customers to run tabs. Problems arose when customers lost money in stocks. Prostitutes were the last to receive what was owed them.

Rosa has evidently sent Jack a "kind" reminder that it's time for him to pay up. His cane will not suffice for payment. Jack blames the drop in stocks both for his inability to pay Rosa and for failing to visit her.

It is important to note, that Jack, as other writers; refers to Rosa as "little Rose" or "little one," making it obvious that Rosa May was a small woman.

In Jack's letter we first come across Rosa's deep distrust of men. "I see in your last, your natural distrust of me shows up." Rosa had reasons to distrust Jack, as an analysis of his handwriting clearly showed. Rosa's involvement with unstable and untrustworthy men is a recurring theme throughout the letters. Her need to choose such men will be explained later.

"I think sometimes you mean what you say and it's but fast for you to reciprocate," hints that Rosa's kind note was also angry and demanding. Rosa's hot temper, her cutting tongue and impulsiveness is revealed here and in other letters.

The Ophir Mine was a large producing mine in Virginia City in 1876. "They have knocked the damn hell out of it here," refers to the manipulation of all Virginia City mining stocks by San Francisco stock brokers, who were called, "Bears."

In July, 1876, the Bears believed the price of Consolidated Virginia and California Mine stocks, the richest Comstock mines, to be over priced. And, they suspected Mackay, Fair and Flood, mine owners, of unloading their own stocks.

In an effort to drive stocks down, the Bears, led by Keene, a broker, began a savage attack on the Consolidated Virginia and California stocks, disregarding the fact that these mines were breaking records in amounts of ore milled, resulting in great profits. Why, in one month, March 1876, these mines produced $3,634,218! Stocks were worth every bit they were being sold for.

But the Bears continued their attack, managing to drive stocks down, depressing the market. Con. Virginia stock dropped from $440 to $240 a share; California, $90 to $65. With the Bonanza mine stocks driven down, other stocks fell, including the Ophir, which evidently Jack had bought into.

A few notes about the Virginia City mines: their greatest yield was 1874-80, though the mines were worked from the 1860's to present. In 1876 it was not known how far the great body of silver ore went. As far as it had been explored, it was city blocks wide and deep. Some believed that the silver ore was inexhaustible.

By 1877, the extent of the ore was known. It was not inexhaustible. Though 1877 was the greatest year of production for the mines, it was ironically a year of economic depression and poverty for the citizens of Virginia City. Many miners lost jobs and were unable to feed their families. From 1878 on, silver production in the Comstock mines dropped year by year and stocks naturally fell with the decline.

The following is the first of the many letters written by Ernest Marks, Rosa's long time lover. This first létter was not written to Rosa, but to a prostitute we will simply know as Jennie. It's doubtful that this is the same woman, Jennie Moore, who ran a brothel in Carson at Third and Ormsby.

Whenever Marks refers to "the Doctor," he is speaking of his penis. The term reflects Marks' vanity, that his sexual prowess is capable of doctoring any woman's sexual needs.

Ernest Marks was twenty-three when he wrote this letter.

Rolands Lake Tahoe
July 7, 1878

My Dear Jennie

Your two letters are at hand this day-as luck would have it I opened the dizy one first-it made me feel funny to see and you can't tell how quick I knew that you had been on a dizy spell but when I opened no. 2 Oh! how glad I was to see my darling was her self once more her dear lady likeself —

I have just arrived. The pop and gin and the medicine are here all o.k. and I now hope I shall be as sound as a roach [Marks may have had a venereal disease.]

I have had a very nice time since I left. I have caught a great many of the speckled beauties and had around 50 in a pen— the thing busted and let them out and for two or three days the wind blew so hard that I could not catch enough to eat— So today we left Camp Starvation as I called it. This week on the 4th I fished all day and only got enough to eat but I hope Monday I shall be able to get a lot to send home to Ed and Taylor so that my baby can also have a mess I don't know how soon I will be able to write again. I shall try and be home as soon as I get well, if I don't get well I will come home for getting up at night to release the Dr. from a crooked posish is not what it is cracked up to be as it is rather colder here at night than it is in Virginia City but I just grin — Oh! such a grin — but it is not as bad as it was at home and my large left [testicle?] is a thing of the past thank the devil I am writing this by the campfire, so you will excuse the bad writing

Peacock is at Emerald Bay. I saw him yesterday I have seen one or two chances to give the Dr. a chance but he and I do not give it a thought. I suppose a great love of Jennie blinds us to everything else

Tomorrow I shall go to the Glenbrook for provisions— I shall always write you at every opportunity. You can write me same as before and if I don't get them sooner I will later

Old Tom is to much of a d----d fool to take any notice of—and if he is my friend let him conduct himself as such not like a sneak, his natural way of doing

There was a woman said to me yesterday, "Don't you get lonesome when you have no ladies around. "Oh, yes," I said. I could be of no use to her [why?] so I left. Dr. did not show any symptoms of wanting any and I was very glad to see he had not forgotten his Rosa.

I am getting as brown as I can make no..[Indecipherable].. and I have not shaved since I left you— I look rough, so Mountain Jack and Rich call me Wild Bill. I do get a little wild sometimes but quit drinking from tonight till I am more your darling as of yore

..[Indecipherable].. My sister said Ed's hair was all coming out in spots. Ed said in his letter that it is no better. I am sorry if he has taken a dose. All my paper is gone. I shall get more. I will see you in the sweet by and by my love. With lots of love and kiss. I am your Ernie

Marks' rambling letter is confusing. If he and Rosa have a relationship, why does he say, "I suppose a great love of Jennie blinds us to everything else," and later say, "...I was very glad to see that he (Marks' penis) had not forgotten his Rosa,?" It's difficult to determine exactly what Jennie is to Marks.

That she is a prostitute, we can be certain and likely a friend of Rosa's. Whether Jennie and Marks have something going on behind Rosa's back, we do not know. An analysis of Marks' handwriting reveals that he had a tremendous sexual appetite, the kind of man who was constantly thinking of sex, and often frequented brothels. And as for his fidelity, Marks was as true as the wind.

Lake Tahoe is about twenty-five miles from Carson City, high in the Sierras. It seems that Marks has a venereal disease and has gone to the mountains to recuperate. His mentioning of the arrival of medicine, "I shall try and be home as soon as I am well," and "... my large left (testicle?) is a thing of the past," all point to Marks having v.d. Knowing his sexual appetite, when he says, "I could be of no use," to the lonely mountain woman, makes one feel certain that Marks is temporarily out of commission.

According to statistics gathered by Eliot Lord and published in his, **Comstock Mining and Miners,** 1883, an extremely well written and informative book about life in Virginia City; veneral disease was the most frequently treated illness on the Comstock. From 1865 to 1880, the Storey County Hospital claimed record of treating 731 cases of v.d., not including the hundreds of cases not reported or treated elsewhere. Virginia City never had a clinic where prostitutes could be examined and treated. Considering the large numbers of prostitutes and the lack of proper medical care and education, it is a wonder venereal disease did not prevail in epidemic proportions.

Ed, a friend of Marks often mentioned in his letters, seems to also have v.d. "My sister says Ed's hair was all coming out in spots. Ed said in his letter that it is no better. I am sorry if he has taken a dose."

The names mentioned here are often mentioned in Marks' letters. Peacock and Rich are friends. Old Tom, is most likely Tom Reynolds, who ran a hides and pelt store in Gold Hill and was a frequent customer of Rosa's.

Marks mentions his drinking problem here and throughout the letters. He was an alcoholic.

All men along the Comstock drank enormous quantities of liquor. There were a hundred saloons in Virginia City, thirty-seven in Gold Hill. After a time, most men were able to devour huge quantities of liquor and not feel it. The Comstock possessed Victorian customs and it was considered unmanly for one to lose control under the influence.

This letter proves that Marks and Rosa knew each other as early as July 7, 1878. They did not meet each other in Bodie as Ella Cain claims.

Another letter from Ernest Marks, his first to Rosa May:

Gold Hill
Dec. 20, 1878

Dearest One,
    Many thanks for your loveing letter of the 19th. I always feel so happy when I hear from you. But so blue when I know I cannot come or be with my Rosa my baby— the time passes very slowly when you are not with me— I don't see any fun— and how, I miss my pet at night no one knows except poor me I am still going hungry [without sex] and I suppose I will till I see my pet. It seems as though every man woman and child knew of you and I. I get it from some

quarter every day. And it makes me feel so bad sometimes that I hardly know what to do. I feel very desperate just now any ways no money, no friends but one, besides my baby

I am thinking myself that I am going to lose my pay— it will be a $122 tonight. I am agoing up to see Tom about it to see if he got any letter from the president yet. If I don't get it I can't get my little one her presents as I had not enough to pay for them— but we still live in hope

I took in the show last night and thought Tom was in for a bad scrape once while he was taking his girl home. That fellow is tough but Tom stood him off— But Donnie is afraid of Jack though she told him to keep away last night. If there had been a scrape I should have been into it as I think it is time someone else has a chance to do a little f---ing in this town beside the so called sports— I guess Jack will let Tom alone now as he had the worst of the bargain last night

I hope you will be careful and not let yourself be bilked [cheated] any more. Charles Boscowitz is a married man, as I am acquainted with his wife— or I may be mistaken it may be his brothers or someone else's wife of the same name but I rather think it is his, I am not certain but you will find it out soon enough if you don't know it now. [Evidently Boscowitz cheated Rosa out of money. Marks may be hinting here, that if Boscowitz has a wife, Rosa could blackmail him, which was common among prostitutes.] Don't you forget it I shall see without anyone knowing it that Dora hears of her Peter Damn them, they would give me away if they could but I don't propose to break my baby's heart by going around with the dizy girls and boys. I am now good and keep away from them all. And good I shall be and save it all for my sweet so that I "Shall be able" when I meet her again— I hope it may be soon and I know you do

I saw Jim Breen on the street last night and he told me Mollie O'Neil had gone to Carson on the evening train. There was no love there. He was still in the street he said... [Marks loses his thoughts.]

Your bird is singing pretty as I write this. The old lady wanted to give him a name— but I told her that he would soon be gone — and then he would get a new name

I am glad to think Em [Emma] did not try my pet. I expect to hear if I get among the boys and girls that you had a lover but I won't believe it as I know my Rosie loves her baby don't you darling [This may imply that Emma made a pass at Rosa. From here it would seem that Marks fears that Rosa has a lesbian lover, and perhaps has had one in the past. Prostitutes often turned to each other for affection, having been mauled by men day after day.]

I shall be off to see Tom soon— I guess Reynolds will be down about Christmas—so Oily Gammon tells me. With great love and a million kiss— I am your Erni

Ernest Marks' first letter to Rosa in Carson City, was written at a time of economic depression along the Comstock Lode. The end of the Great Bonanza was now in sight. Only the Bonanza mines were profitable and able to keep miners employed. The majority of the mines had closed down or had levied assessments on stock holders. Many miners were unemployed and grubbed for whatever work available to support their hungry families. Begging in the streets by widows and orphans was common. Two bit saloons became bit saloons, businesses went bankrupt or were forced to move elsewhere. The outlook for all was gloomy. The miners and various merchants had put their complete trust in the mines. Once thought inexhaustible, the mines were now giving out. All were dismayed.

The question arises while reading Marks' letter, that if he missed Rosa as much as he says he does, why didn't he live in Carson City nearer to her? Or, why didn't he visit her more often? Carson City was a two hour train trip from Virginia City. The trip took so long because of the lengthy switch-backs down the mountains to Carson.

Marks did not visit Rosa more often perhaps for two reasons: one, he probably didn't have the train fare. Second, assuming Marks worked during the day, he would have had to visit Rosa at night, during Rosa's working hours. Not good for Rosa's business nor Marks' vanity.

In the first paragraph we learn that others know about Marks and Rosa. Marks is not happy about this. In fact, he's ashamed that people know that he is romantically involved with a prostitute. His shame reflects his guilt which often seeps from his letters. There is little doubt that men in the saloons he frequents have been razzing him about Rosa. "I get it from some quarter every day. And it makes me feel so bad sometimes that I hardly know what do do."

The pay of a $122 Marks fears he may lose, was quite a sum considering miners made $4 a day for eight hours of grueling work, $20 a week, $80 a month, and $4 a day at this time was top money.

Marks, as I've said, was obsessive regarding sex as well as an alcoholic. He hung around the red light dives and saloons with a group of men who befriended the local prostitutes. Some of these men were miners; others, pimps or men who lived off the earnings of prostitutes.

Marks often refers to these people as the "dizy girls and boys." "...I don't propose to break my baby's heart by going around with all the dizy girls and boys. I am now good and keep away from them all." Rosa, evidently, knew that Marks hung around with other prostitutes and pimps when he was away from her. When he did so, she knew he drank and had relations with other prostitutes. Though Rosa bartered her body daily to many men, ironically she expected Marks to be monogamous, something he was simply not capable of. His strong sexual appetite needed to be fed often and with many different women. Though he defends himself here and claims that he is "now good," one can be certain, his recent celibacy will not last long.

Tom, most likely the Tom of the last letter and evidently working for the same company, has not yet heard from the president concerning the workers pay. The "president" is most likely the president of the mining company Marks and Tom were working for. Many of the smaller mining companies did not know from one month to the next if they would be able to make payroll. Marks, it appears, is now suffering from their financial insecurity, as were many men.

Marks often refers to Rosa as his "pet," his "little girl," his "baby." Such expressions give the impression that Rosa was someone he considered needed to be taken care of, that Marks was her protector. From other letters, it seems the opposite case, Rosa being the stronger one looking out for Marks.

Donnie, the woman Tom and Jack fought over, was a prostitute. Jack, maybe the man who was involved with Rosa.

Charles Boscowitz was the brother of Frank Boscowitz, 27, who ran a successful clothing store on North Carson Street in Carson City. Evidently, Charles Boscowitz cheated Rosa out of money, something that is often happening to her.

Dora was a prostitute and Peter, her pimp.

Jim Breen was at this time a miner, became a Virginia City policeman, and finally ran the U.S. Saloon in Virginia City 1887-88. His girl, Molly O'Neil, sometimes called Margaret, was a prostitute.

Ernest Marks:

Gold Hill
Dec 27, 1878

My Own Rosa,

Your promised and very loving letter I am most thankful to received this day— thank you darling. I am always so happy to hear from you. Today I am feeling fine only I am so nervous that I can hardly write I drink so little now I suppose is the reason but I feel better for it and I look ever so much better. I was in Virginia last night till 10 oclock when I was coming home I met Dan. "Halow! Dan! I said, how are you

Deacon, he said. I went on. But he turned, I say! I was redy for I expected trouble. I turned, well I said: Where is Rosa he said — In Carson I have been told, I said. Yes, I heard she was there he says, but she will starve there. I don't know I am certain, I said, but I hope not. "She went out of town broke," he says. Yes, I remarked, I was told the same thing. I had a row with her but I tried to make it right by offering her $40 — but she was to stubborn she did not get a cent. I should have given her a $100 if she had taken the $40 by God I was going to do it, no mistake but she put it on a little too thick, but she is the best little woman I ever mett no mistake and it was not her fault, it was that s of a b— Mollie O'Neil— the dirty b— just let me meet her g-d her, for if I don't fix her — He had plenty of opportunitys I guess but I did not say so I came very near telling him if he thought so much of you, he might send you some money now but thought I had better not He says Mollie O'Neil is in Carson to. **It was all news to me** so I led him to believe and I don't care weather he believes it or not. I think he is drinking — he looks that way and acts kind of stupid I guess he feels it I hope he may the brute Yes, as you say, God speed all travelers. I may see him in Bode [Bodie?] as I have an application for a situtation out there. What my prospects are I don't know yet. My watching job has petered out. I have a $100 coming. I shall soon be among the mash [unemployed.]

I have a new suit making. I shall go up to try on the coat this evening, a new hat, a pair of $12 shoes. I shall be looking creditable to my Rosa when I come down. What do you say? Your bird is singing so pretty today. You will be surprised when you see him you will think its Erni alive again

I suppose you leave yourself out to count Em in among the six beauties — Well love you are handsomer in my eyes than any one I know

It is very cold here now at night. I shall tell Oily Gammon what you said — he sends his regards to you. I suppose you have seen Reynolds by this time. Gammon is very attentive to his Donnie, he is there every evening now he tells me— he is as badly stuck as I am after my darling But God ain't he jealous, the old fool— She calls him Papa

I got a wall pocket for Christmas. I am glad you were pleased with my presents to you. I am glad to here Miss Jennie and Em liked you so well as to give you a present, but they don't think one half as much as I do my baby. I shall be down soon I hope but I don't know where Ormsby Street is— so you must tell me as near as you can— and which may the numbers run so that I may find you if I come— if I come I say— but you bet I will come if I am not dead before I am redy I shall bring you the bird to You might meet me if it not to far and the weather permitin I suspect it will snow soon again— My gov is down sick again his old chum rheumatism is with him — and he has got the Gov on his back but it is not bad however— Christmas whiskey is the cause I guess— he was well till Ed gave him some money that did the business—

Peacock still lives and is as fat as ever —Ed sent for his girl from your town yesterday and I guess they are angry at one another— She is to much of a flirt, Ed should not complain as he got in his work and it cost him very little— He and his red headed girl are all ok again— so I am told. I guess I am the virtuous one of all the boys now— Oily Gammon says it will be like a new married couple when you and Rosa meet again—When do you go, he said I told him I did not know He got his girl some presents I will tell you about it when I see you— don't you hope it will be soon, I do— I also have a good joke to tell you on Bob when I see you, he told me of it yesterday— I had a good laugh at him I have no more to write so I shall be off to town— Love and Kiss for my own darling— as ever Your loving and affectionate Emi

A week since his last letter, Marks is in better spirits though he is soon to be unemployed. He is on the wagon now. His nervousness is evidence of his severe alcohol problem. Rosa, as you will see, was always encouraging Marks to keep away from drink. This may have been for his own good, or to have kept him away from other whores.

Marks' clever description of his meeting with Dan reveals quite a bit about Rosa. She has left town broke. Another customer has failed to pay up. Dan owes Rosa $140 but offers her $40. Her pride offended, Rosa explodes and gives Dan a good verbal licking which earns Dan's respect.

But Marks does not defend Rosa. He knows nothing of her affairs. Marks wants to keep his relationship with Rosa secret. He is sensitive to criticism as an analysis of his handwriting proves.

"I suppose you leave yourself out to count Em (Emma) among the six beauties." Rosa is working at Jennie Moore's house with six other girls. Rosa does not consider herself pretty though we know from her photo that she was very much so. This is the first hint of Rosa's lack of self-esteem.

Tom Reynolds, Gold Hill hides and pelt man and frequent customer, has been to Carson for his weekly visit to Rosa.

Oily Gammon, an older man and friend of Marks', is now devoting his nights to Donnie, the prostitute Tom and Jack nearly fought over.

Rosa has only recently moved to Carson. Marks has not visited her there yet and does not know where Ormsby Street is; the red light. He asks Rosa to give directions. He will bring her pet bird.

The "gov" is Marks' father, who has rheumatism— and an alcohol problem.

Ed, Marks' good friend, is seeing red headed Mable Grey, a notorious prostitute.

Marks still feigning his virtue to Rosa.

Gold Hill, Nevada
Dec. 30, 1878

My Darling,

Many thanks for your loveing letter today of the 28, it was the one I expected yesterday— Yes dear I was very nervous, but I am sorry to think that you do not believe that I had not been drinking after me telling you I had not, but it is usual no one thinks me capable of a good action   I shall take the game as well as the name, though I have entirely quit

The grand change has been terrible I have been lost and not myself at all

Last night I was in Virginia and went down C St with two school girls   I saw Dan and he took it all in one was in black and I guess he kind of thought it was you, but you would make two of that little dame   I guess I shall find the house without any trouble, when I come down. I guess I should have found it any how with much trouble   Reynolds is still here he told Oily Gammon that he, Reynolds, would go down this week but though Reynolds has plenty of money he hates to give it up, though he appears to be pretty badly stuck after you. There is nothing new. You can expect me this week— I don't feel like writing any more now should like to write a long letter but I am disgusted and blue everything is going wrong again today with me   I guess I shall get my money next month   Ed and Gammon are OK   I am all anxiety to see my love-by-by Love and kiss

yours always,

Emi

Written three days since his last letter, this gives you an idea how frequently Marks and Rosa wrote each other. Though recently invented, telephones were not in general use and telegrams were too expensive. Letters were the only means of communication for the lovers some twenty miles apart.

Though Marks has claimed in several letters that he is being good and staying on the wagon, Rosa, an intelligent girl, knows Marks all too well. Soon as pressures mount, Marks will be drinking.

Marks himself claims that, "no one thinks me capable of a good action." His failures weighed heavily upon him. One feels him struggling to do more with his life, but his failures drive him back to drink. His poor self-image sticks with him, a shadow he cannot shake. He is soon to visit his girl friend at a Carson City whorehouse.

The following letter is from a Mrs. Carr, written after the recent news of her daughter's death:

New York
Jan, 4th, 1879

Miss Rosa May
        My dear Friend-
I was sorry to hear of my poor childs death and thank you very kindly for answering my letter.

        I am very glad her body was not opened but I would like to know the cause of her death-

        I thank you and the other ladies for the kind interest you have taken in my daughter and God bless you all for your kindness

        I did not receive your letter till yesterday and it was a sad blow to me   I feel heart broken— I am very glad to know there is going to be a stone on her grave

        If I only had the means I would love to go on and see her body now but I haven't the means to do so

        You said if you could get any further information you would let me know. I shall be very thankful to hear anything that concerns my poor daughter or anything that belonged to her and may God reward you for all your kindness to me. If there is any thing there belonging to her that would be valuable to me as keepsakes if you could send them on I would be grateful

        Direct a letter to Mrs. Carr
        180 West 10th Street, New York

If you would send me the address of the woman with whom she boarded I could write her and find out the particulars about her sickness   It is very singular what ailed her   I would like to kow what caused her death

I thank you again for your kindness and close

your grateful friend
Mrs. Carr

My daughter's name was Mamie Nenninger

Mrs. Carr's thankful letter is one of several indications that Rosa May was kind hearted.

Some time in December, 1878, a friend of Rosa's died. She was a prostitute and may have died from one of the many venereal diseases.

Rosa's kind letter to Mrs. Carr, brought good news to the grieved mother that Rosa and other prostitutes had pitched in for a stone to mark her daughter's grave. Rosa did not know what the dead girl's real name was and was forced to ask her mother. Most prostitutes went under an assumed name. We do not know whether Mrs. Carr knew that her daughter, Mamie Nenninger, was a prostitute.

Mrs. Carr's letter was addressed to Rosa May, 18 South D Street, Cad Thompson's brothel. Rosa must have gone back to Virginia City from Carson when she learned of Mamie's death. This leads one to assume that Mamie died in Virginia City. However; a search of death records in the Virginia City courthouse showed no record of death for any woman in December, 1878. I spent 2½ hours under a broiling August sun searching the Virginia City cemetery for Mamie Nenninger's grave but I did not find it.

Another letter from Ernest Marks, addressed to Rosa in Carson City:

At Home [Gold Hill]
Sunday Jany 5, 1879

Rosa Darling,

Now I shall answer your loveing letter of the 2 inst. Yes, I thought the card rather neat and it was so ... [Indecipherable] ... during the day and you were pleased.

Yes love I am a good boy and shall try to be. No! Pet I did-not get into some girls box, but Tom did-Donnie gave him that paper and I wrote that letter in his room and he gave me that paper. Oh! no! my Rosa, rather say that I am a conventient article for Uncle Tom [he may mean Tom Reynolds] Oh! no I can't have it that way for I do not want you to think that I am giving you traffic [business] so I don't wish you to say you suppose it is all **right,** when I know baby mine that though you say it is all right you feel in your darn good heart that you mean it is all wrong. No! No! Rosa if I should do anything wrong Oily Gammon would only be the first to tell it to someone so that you could hear it.

I have not got my new suit yet. The taylors all got drunk so I was disappointed in not getting it as soon as I expected it. But I hope to get them this week and then darling if my new job has given out please look out for your baby. My new business keeps me busy- but I guess it will not last much longer I can't say that I am stuck after it but it will get a few dollars.

New Years I had my black suit on and I looked so, I was often told during the day, real **sweet** and nice. I got on very nice did not get tight Three drinks was all I took during the day and I felt good the next morning

Last night I took in Vovoneys Sorrie and had rather a pleasant time. I guess you have seen the long expected Reynolds by this time as he left here the other day to go to Reno and I heard him say that he was going to stay in Carson two days and then agoing to San Francisco.

Ed has his red headed darling down here at some rooms up town. [Red heads were considered best in bed.] She came down last night and stayed with him and is still there and will go back tonight. She is rather pleasant. I met her today when I returned from the p.o. [post office] I was disappointed in not getting a letter from you today- ByBy darling bless my baby Sweet Kisses Write soon your loving Emi

It is difficult to ascertain what code of ethics or morality, if any, that Rosa and Marks lived by. We know that Rosa has accused Marks of getting in some girls "box." Rosa does not want Marks sleeping with other women. Nor does she like the idea of him sending her "traffic," business.

Evidently, Rosa has told Marks, "If it's alright for you to send me your friends, it's alright for me to take their money." She is testing Marks love. Marks plays along. "I don't wish you to suppose it is all **right**, when I know baby mine that you mean it is all wrong."

Marks is still living in Gold Hill and has a new job. We do not know what kind of work it is.

As always, Marks is defensive about his drinking, claiming he's only had three drinks New Year's Day. Unlike other lovers, Marks and Rosa did not spend Christmas nor New Year's together.

Tom Reynolds has made his visit to Rosa.

Ed and Mable Grey are together again. Ed keeping Mable in rooms away from his and Marks' place.

The following letter from Marks was addressed to Rosa at No. 1 Ormsby Street, Carson City:

January 7, 1879
Gold Hill
Oh You Darling,

You don't know how glad I was this evening to hear from you. I was very much disappointed in not getting a letter from you yesterday but I suppose you're never too busy to write.

My love, your letter sounds as though you feel hurt. It is so unlike you. I'm sorry to see you feeling as you do and I think it is unkind of you to feel that way towards me for though you may think because I do not answer your letters as promptly as usual that I'm off on something else I can tell you darling that there is nothing in it and I do hope darling one you will believe to be of old your Ernest and no one else's for I have not since you have gone had anything to do with woman or single girl or married, widow or grass widow [a woman divorced or separated from her husband] or woman of any kind. This may seem strange to you who knows me so well but it is the truth as sure as I write this The doctor [his penis] seems to think of no one else but his Rosa's doctoress [you can guess]. And as for taking interest or pleasure in my new job, I cannot see where the pleasure comes to wrangle all day with creditors and their bills. I thought my job would end last week. I was to be paid ten dollars for writing up a small set of books that they thought would take me two days. I did it in only one and then they wanted me to stay and take in the money and I am still at it for you know what few dollars I get I very much need.

I might have come down to see you Sunday but I should have had to be back Sunday night. What good would that have been? I thought more so I stayed at home but now have an idea of coming down Saturday night with the horse and back Monday. If I do I will let you know before I come if you say that I may come.

Reynolds was in your house last night but you were engaged and he left. He went to San Francisco tonight. He told Oily Gammons that the house was doing a land office business and he did not want to get a wet dick.

I am sorry that I was not on the train Friday to meet my love but I hope you will think no harm in it and not feel hard toward your baby for I meant not to fool you and would not willingly disappoint my pet for any consideration. Why Rosa do you say good-bye, no more love and kisses for me and you wish to be [indecipherable] sometimes.

For today there is no hard task
No burden that I would not bear with grace
No sacrifice I could name or ask
That were granted could I see your sweet face

Oh Rosa how can you think for a moment that good-bye. Remember we sometimes should not [indecipherable] felt by me. Pet I donot write to you in any such strain but my love I know you do not mean it. Millions of kisses and lodes of love

Ernest

The pimp or boyfriend of a prostitute was the most important human being in her superficial life. He was someone she could turn to, someone she could share the troubles of her work, someone she could at times receive love and support from. Rosa chose Ernest Marks to be that important person in her life, although he was unstable, untrustworthy and not able to give of himself.

Marks and Rosa are quarreling. She has scolded him for not writing promptly. Rosa is hurt and feels that Ernest has made a fool of her by not coming to Carson the previous Friday when he was supposed to. She is worried that his new job is taking him away from her. And, she fears that Marks is sleeping with other women, the supreme rejection.

By not coming to see her, by not writing and sleeping with other women, Rosa feels uneasy about their relationship. Fearing that Ernest will soon reject her, Rosa breaks off with Ernest.

But Marks plays innocent. It is unlike her to be hurt, he says. He has not slept with anyone else. His job is of no great importance and he will come down Saturday and stay till Monday. He pleads with her, writes four lines of poetry and asks her forgiveness. He does not seem to fear that her anger will last. He knows Rosa.

Reynolds was down to see Rosa Saturday night. Rosa's brothel is doing great business.

February 5, 1879
Gold Hill
Darling Rosa,

    your long expected letter is here at last. I am so glad I should not have had time to answer it today but I was down here to see some parties against whom I had some bills. You don't know how glad I am to receive your letter. It is very short but I suppose there is no scandal in you being busy. I'm glad to hear that times are getting better with you and I hope that they will keep on improving with my baby.

    I should judge from reading your letter that you had a drinking party at your house. [Indecipherable] I wrote you yesterday which note I suppose you have today, I began to feel anxious thinking that your prospects [indecipherable] had happened. I came very near to passing in my chips the other night but today I'm all o.k. except that my neck is just a little stiff and my head and [indecipherable].

    If this beautiful weather keeps on I must try and get down and see you Sunday. I took in Ed's shooting gun and got some rabbits [indecipherable] has been sick only Gammon and I have been able to see Also he and that dame have been living in town together I believe. Ed still has got his red headed girl. She is going to move into Molly Ashton's today and there will be three or four more for the boys today. Ed says that his baby tells him that Weston pays his girls to sell wine for him. Ed I guess is trying to get me away from my pet. I suppose he thinks I need a little but I don't unless I get it from my baby.

    Love and kisses for my dearest Rosa.

                    Emi

    It has been a month since Marks' last letter. He is a bill collector.

    Rosa's letter is short. Marks doesn't mind nor does he mind that business is picking up for Rosa. She is having more men and making more money. "I'm glad to hear that times are getting better with you..."

Marks' friend, Oily Gammon and his girl, Donnie are living together. Mable Grey, the infamous, is still with Ed. Mable soon to be working at Molly Ashton's brothel, along with three or four new girls.

Weston, probably the owner of a brothel, pays her girls to sell wine, a common custom.

Marks still feigning his virtue.

February 11, 1879
Gold Hill

My Own Darling,

Thanks to you and the railroad here I am again. I had six minutes to spare when I got to the train. I'm not feeling very bright today my head is hurting me again. I saw Oily and his girl today. They are fine it seems. Ed was sorry he returned home but thought it was better because his strawberry blonde might find it out. It looks like a storm here today, the wind is blowing pretty hard. The wind Saturday night in Virginia [indecipherable] It did not storm here like it did in your town.

McGrath was caught in bed with Mrs. Noel Crowell, a dressmaker and milkman on C Street and got kicked out by her husband. He is ole Beecher and I have known him for a long time. Man is frail and only a man but Mrs. Noel Crowell   Oh, such taste but they are something of [indecipherable] but only for their bad looks and she more than he for her gin pressing habits. That little red headed dame came up at the train. I guess she belongs at the [indecipherable]

My Dad is feeling better and is now getting about the house a little and managed to get a clean shave yesterday so he is looking pretty well. I hope you are over your fright. I guess it is all o.k.

The doctor seems himself but it is not time for him but I am not at all uneasy about him. He is such a [indecipherable] I am not about to [indecipherable]
love and kisses,
Emi

Marks has been down to see Rosa in Carson City. She has paid his train fare back to Gold Hill. They have been drinking, Marks is hung over.

Oily and Donnie are fine but Ed's sneaking around on Mable.

Marks referring to his penis, "I am not at all uneasy about him," probably means that he has not caught disease from Rosa.

February 15, 1879
Gold Hill

My love,
your dear kind and loving letter I am in receipt of today. Thank you darling for being so prompt in answering my letters. Yes I did ride [possiby write] to San Francisco to get a place but not for me but for a friend who in former days was superintendent of mines here. I wrote to him to see if he could get me a place somewhere. I did not ask him to get it in any particular camp or place only so I got a situation. God forgive me Rosa, its breaking my heart to sit here doing nothing and you in that damn town. I want to take you out of it or help you along.

I am told that Reynolds was engaged to that young lady in Empire but it is all moon knocked in the head and that they are seven. It was by some married woman in Virginia and he has also got himself into another scrape so I was told. There is a married woman in Virginia Oily Gammons, Johny Hobart, John Strammon, Henry Gusten and Reynolds have got to. Reynolds was the last of all. She's now 4 months

111

in the family way and she says it was Tom Reynolds who done it. Anyway she said she will make him pay for it so Gammons says.

No Oily has not got that money. I was told in Virginia that it would be here in a few days to pay all hands. And yes you are right dear, he is Oily Gammons, but he better not ever do anything of that kind. Stone cutting at Carson has no charms for Oily Gammons. It is an old saying, love is blind but darling it is not in this case of ours.

Many thanks for your pretty and appropriate Valentine. No post mark on it but I know it is from you. Mother is going to give me a frame to put it in. I send you one. I saw some pretty ones but my bank account has gone where the woodbine twineth.

I guess Ed and his dame will soon quit. He's getting his eyes opened. You are right, they do not love as we do. In fact she is only a money getting creature and that is all she thinks of I can't say I like her at all. She has too much deceit in her to suit me. She is not like my baby. Oh you darling.

> For this belief whatever betide
> Though friends prove false and court each eye
> At morn and noon when night's set free
> I'll fondly love, bless and think of thee Rose

> I give all my love and kisses to my darling.
> Always thine baby.
>   Emest

Marks is again out of work, unable to send Rosa a Valentine's card. He is living with his father and mother. Has just written someone in San Francisco for jobs for himself and an old friend, once a mine superintendent. A superintendent was a position of great responsibility and good pay. The superintendent oversaw the workings of the entire mine often deciding which way a drift or stope should run.

Marks is seeking work elsewhere as the depression becomes greater along the Comstock and more men are laid off.

Ernest does seem to be genuinely concerned for Rosa when he says, "God forgive me Rosa, its breaking my heart to sit here doing nothing and you in that damn town. I want to take you out of it or help you along."

That "damn town," of course, was Carson City, a jumping off place for travelers heading south to the recent boom camp of Bodie, or north to Reno and San Francisco. Many were leaving Virginia City and going to Bodie through Carson. Each day, the stages left Carson full of passengers for Bodie. They were followed by twenty horse teams hauling great mining equipment to the boom camp. With so many travelers passing through town, Carson City was more profitable for Rosa than Virginia.

Carson City was then a town of five to seven thousand people. Many were employed by the Carson and Tahoe Lumber Company, a mile south of the red light. Its great yard was a mile long and half a mile wide. A twelve mile flume from Spooner's Summit, carried the newly cut timber down from the Sierras to Carson. This wood was used in the Virginia City and Gold Hill mines which had already consumed millions of board feet. Cities of timbers lay beneath these two camps.

The Carson City Mint, several blocks from the red light, employed many men. Others found work in Empire City, a suburb north of Carson along the Carson River where stamp mills and saw mills were located. And of course there were travelers. It was from these men that Rosa and other prostitutes earned their livings.

It seems Marks' family lived in Gold Hill. He has mentioned his father, a sister and now his mother. He also had a brother, Morris, who opened a wholesale liquor business in Bodie in 1880. Ernest later worked for him.

From this letter it seems that Rosa and Ernest were able to love one another. They must have had something. They were together off and on for thirty-five years.

Gold Hill
1879

My Dear Rosa,

What is the matter? You are not sick I hope. I am feeling anxious about you as I should surely. Haven't a letter from you today or yesterday. But I don't know what's the matter with my pet.

I am unable to work anymore, I am sick. I took a fall which has laid me up today but I am up again. My neck and head feel funny. Reynolds to Em kindness and best wishes. Good luck and lots of luck. I am always yours. Love and kisses. Emi.

April 17, 1879
Gold Hill

Dear Rosa,

you dear loving girl, your letter is here all o.k. and I have perused it. I must say that I was correct in calling you a bad guesser for I had put it up that you were only guessing. As I said before there is nothing in it. I don't let them bother me at all.

I see by this morning's paper that Alex Crane and Dora Eliot got married on the 15th in Virginia. Good enough. And that Robert Hill Lindsay has got to Annie Baugerman by marrying her at the residence of her poppa and mamma and it goes as it layest. I hope it may be a success. Bob has worked at that thing a good long time now but I can't say I admire his taste at all. She's rather smart and pleasant but homely but then its nice to have a little. I can't say she has any unless its below her chin.

Tonight, tomorrow night and the next night we shall have the Bergois in the opera house. As usual, I don't go, I have seen them before 2 or 3 times, that is enough.

Ed received yesterday three pictures of his Mabel all in different positions and they look well. I must say she appears to be in very good health. He is very much tickeled over them. I made a [indecipherable] The five pictures are different. Just think of it.

Peter Saltry [possibly Faltry or Daltry] as well as Bell Saltry has got the grand bounce. It seems it was Miss Peel the homely that he thought himself so solid with, in fact all the losers got the grand.

Peel has got herself another fellow, by the name of Terry a soft fool. Peter and Bell Saltry would have had a fight night before last if it nad not been for [undecipherable] Both made it up we don't care. Saltry's are N.G. and don't forget it.

I send you the china [money.] You just bet I am a good boy and all my love and kisses belong to Rosa. Regards to Em. I am always your wild dutchman.   Ernie.

Rosa has perhaps said in her last letter, that she feels Ernest is troubled by the opinions of others regarding their relationship. But Ernest defends himself, "I don't let them bother me," which could not have been true. Marks was sensitive to criticism. Rosa here, using her fine intuition.

Alex Crane was an assistant foreman at the Ophir Mine, 1873-74. It was a position of good pay and responsibility. In 1875 he was a teamster and lived on South D Street near the red light. In 1883-84 he was a shaftman for the C and C and lived in a lodging house at 8 North C Street.

Robert Hill Lindsay, Jr., was the son of Robert Hill Lindsay, City Attorney for Virginia City, and one of the original forty-niners.

Mabel has sent Ed nude pictures of herself.

Peter and Bell Saltry, low-lifes, were thrown out of town.

April 22, 1879
Gold Hill

Rosa Darling,

       your dear kind and loving letter I received yesterday. I know my pet that you are disappointed this morning that I did not answer it as soon as I received it. But I was to have something to do yesterday by making an appearance in Virginia. I was there nearly all day but as my usual luck I did not get it. So baby of mine I hope you will excuse my not having written you.

       I did not see those dizzy dames from your city   I guess China Charlie knows what he is talking about when he says the girls are making nothing. It is fearful dull and the boys are in the same boat as the girls. They don't appear to have a cent or are hardly making anything.

       Cino is working for Tom Duncan and Joe Gavin. He appears to be very steady. I never see him with a cut mouth at all. He appears to be having a good close game of it now and I like many others, are glad of it. The certainty [?] bis has not started yet. Benster, Joe, George Green and some others besides Petro are not going to work it. I don't know how it will go as there is a law against it in this state.

       Matt Canavan's underground party was a grand thing about 100 people attended. Ed took a girl. He and Brad drank wine out of goblets. There was plenty of it and I was told it was rather a jolly crowd after supper. They danced till 4 o'clock Sunday morning. I don't think Mrs. Canavan went to church as usual that morning, Cutt Mouth [indecipherable] nor Jim Sheridan went there. Pete Dunn and more of the gang were there however.

       Weather is fine today but Saturday night and Sunday fearful cold and windy. There don't seem to be as many people in town as usual. I [indecipherable]. I hear Weston is going to have some new girls soon and Cad Thompson also. I don't see why, there appears to be too many now. I'm sorry to hear my baby that you are falling back but you are in better luck than most of them it seems.

Jack Brady was asking about you yesterday. I told him you were fine the last time I saw you, about a month ago. It is getting to be a long time my girl. I keep trying to make a piece but it seems I can't. Forever like you dear self, I live in hopes of better times.

I had quite a talk with Dan the other day. I started it but he never mentioned your name. He was on horse back going to Gold Hill he said.

With my best wishes. I am only yours. Regards to Emma.

> Emi

Hard times along the Comstock. There are too many prostitutes in Virginia City and they are not making enough. The men, like the women, do not have much money. Rosa is making less and complains of it.

Throughout this period, Virginia City's, **Territorial Enterprise,** carried increasing numbers of brawls in saloons. Many were arrested for drunk and disorderly conduct, the highest crime in the camp. With more men laid off, frustrations exploded into brawling.

Tom Duncan, 37, was a gambler.

Whatever Benster, Joe Gavin, George Green and Petro are up to, it is illegal. Crime increased with the bad times.

Matt Canavan was a superintendent of the New York mine, a lesser mine. Jim Sheridan was a miner. Pete Dunn, an Irishman, was a bartender in 1875, had his own saloon in 1880-81 and became Storey County Assessor 1883-84.

Weston, evidently ran a brothel. She and Cad Thompson are to have some new girls.

Jack Brady, may be the Jack of an earlier letter. Checking his name, I learned there were two in Virginia City, one a miner; the other, a teamster.

Gold Hill
June 3, 1879

Dear Rosa,
       Your very welcome letter came to hand yesterday evening. I was so glad to see that it was your old self who wrote it. I am real glad to know that you are enjoying the boss blessing— good health. I wish I could say as much. I feel as though I was in the family way and look thin and care worn. I don't know why it should be but it is.
       I feel happy and why shouldn't I, I have such a darling good girl. I will soon be done with my job. It will not turn out as good as I expected. Still, I will get something out of it. It has been a hard job, and raised some blisters I can tell you.
       It is very warm here now and such pretty nights. Last night the moon appeared to have a black eye as in [indecipherable]
       From your letter, Dutch Kate must have good booze again, as she or rather her husband.
       Scotty as usually cared not to keep away from the faro games and it went where the woodbine twineth. Sister Eva is keeping house for Inez I am told. Mable is the only girl in the house who is making room, rent and grub. Oh George, this is a cousin of yours [indecipherable] often mentions one friend [indecipherable] She the grand dame with so many ladies, likes quality, is a beautiful strawberry blonde and to the bargain.
       Ed says Daisy, [indecipherable], Fanny went with some minstrel to Carson on a drunk and I was told that Miss Rouse returned with some new stock also that Tom Simfawcett is now the boss with Inez. Must be a good one or good for nothing, we don't care. Ed and a friend are going to Steamboat next week, Oily Gammons has started his mine up, put on his brother in law, as watchman, in fact he is the only man at it in and about the mine. I guess it will not be as good as it seemed. So as the rough and ready. Regards to Em.[Emma] Love and kisses to my pet.
       Emi.

Nearly two months since Marks' last letter. Difficult to say whether letters written in between this time were lost over the years.

Rosa has recovered from another illness, we do not know what it was.

Dutch Kate was a Carson City madam.

Inez ran a brothel in Virginia City. Mabel is now one of her girls, a boarder, and the "only girl making room rent and grub." Often, girls in a large house were called, "boarders" because they rented a room from the madam. After paying rent, whatever a girl made was hers. This differed from madams who ran houses on a percentage basis, where a girl received only so much for a "trick." Evidently, Inez was using the boarder method.

In efforts to replenish business, madams often changed girls. Those girls who were popular and made good money, stayed on. Those who didn't were shown the door. Prostitutes were entertainers of a sort and they moved around frequently.

Even among prostitutes, there was status. Parlour house girls had the number one position. They were most often the prettiest. They were fed and clothed by the madam and saw the more affluent customers.

Below this was the crib girl, who rented a small two room building for so much a week. After paying rent, whatever the crib girl made was hers.

There were, of course, common street hookers who searched the streets for customers. Compared to the parlour house girl, given protection and comaderie of other girls, the street hooker had it tough. She was open to the worst abuse, theft, beatings and murder. A street hooker became hard in very little time.

Perhaps worst, were the "cow yards." In San Francisco's Barbary Coast, a run down, cut-throat district, there were "cow yards", crummy hotels filled with fifty to a hundred tired prostitutes. Here girls received 25 or 30 cents a trick.

Rosa May at this time was still young. She was twenty-four in 1879, and still pretty enough to be kept on in the Carson and Virginia City whorehouses.

Miss Rouse was another Virginia City madam, evidently has recently brought in new "stock."

Tom Simfawcett is now Inez's pimp and lover.

Steamboat Springs is a hot spring resort in Washoe Valley on the road between Carson City and Reno. Its waters are as hot as they were in Rosa's time. Buildings there date back to the 1870's.

By this letter, we can see that Marks was quite familiar with the camp's various brothels, madams, girls and pimps. So were many of the men living on the Comstock. Marks took particular interest in their doings, due to his desires, and; for Rosa's sake, who might need a place in one of the houses.

June 11, 1879
Gold Hill

Dear Rosa,

when I arrived yesterday I went down to see how my man was getting on which was very slow I must say. I worked a while there, came home and fell asleep. I feel very mean today it is raining and I feel like an iceberg. Ed looked very cross when I got back. I suppose Miss Mabel had to attend to someone else's business as usual not her own but it made no difference for he said nothing. He told Oily Gammons I was a hell of a fellow, which I guess is true enough. I don't know if he will be off on his trip tomorrow or not. I hope he may for I should like to see him away for awhile, away for a few days so he may look more pleasant than he has for some time. That red headed dame is leading him a sorry life of it I think for he is not of yore. But it is not my business for I wouldn't make an example to anyone. He was looking well. I cannot write anymore. I feel miserable. Ed and Bob took over the fish.

love and kisses,
Emie

P.S. I forgot to say that I missed you in the morning, thanks for the same.

Marks has been down to see Rosa. He was up most of the night drinking. He's tired and hung over.

Mabel Grey, the red head, a troublesome woman is leading Ed a sorry life. Ed's as depressed as Marks.

June 12, 1879

Dear Rosa,

I'm happy to acknowledge the safe arrival of your dear kind letter today. Ed, as I said before nothing to you, I judge that Mabel told him about me. From his looks, I guess he and her will soon quit for it is now busted and I was told it was not him but some other fellow who was going to keep her. He was away with a cat last night, one of those Sunday school kind who cheat the regular out of what belongs to them. He is as true and constant to his Mabel as the wind and weather in this country.

I saw George Green and he wanted to know where he knew you, I told him I did not know. He was somewhat bothered about your telling about Viola and Weston being at the picnic. I laughed but never let on that I knew anything about it. Saltry got drunk Monday night and fell down the stairs in one of the houses of joy and has got one of his eyes in mourning to look at in the glass as he stands behind the bar.

I see by the paper this morning that Johnny Hobart is gone to Australia and it reads to me as if Johnny is not the only one in the family that was on it. I may misunderstand it but I would not blame her if she did Hobart [indecipherable], no reason for his departure and she returned to her home in San Francisco. Perhaps she was down there on a visit and he was an unexpected arrival. Be that how it may I don't care for I know how it is myself but I was never like him myself.

I got my job done and now the [indecipherable] but there is little left in it. The doctor, I'm happy to let you know, is well and quite as of yore.

I did not think you cared to get that house for certain. "Our Luck" as usual. Don't you know I'm getting tired of such luck. I'm getting to be a chronic grouch.

Weather beautiful today, very little rain. Regards to Em [Emma]

respectfully yours,

Erni

Marks has blown it. He has fooled around with Mabel, Ed's red head. Ed and Mabel are soon to part and some other man is going to keep her.

Don't know who George Green, Viola nor Johnny Hobart were. Weston, Virginia City brothel owner, mentioned again. Saltry, who in an earlier letter was bounced from town, has fallen down stairs in a Virginia brothel.

Rosa had evidently wanted to rent a certain house in Virginia City. She and Marks have missed their opportunity. Marks complains here, and in other letters about their bad luck.

June 14, 1879
Gold Hill

Dear Rosa,

your dear letter found today as usual. I am very glad to hear that you are enjoying yourself so nicely. If this is a short and poorly written letter please excuse me for I am in a very poor humor.

My damn bad luck follows everyone as well as I. Yesterday as they were milling my stuff there was a rock in it and it broke a pan and caused a loss of $200 to my friend who was working it for me. Damn such luck I say. I expected to get it returned today but now won't until next week.

Ed goes to Tahoe tomorrow by Carson and Glenbrook to Hot Springs. He will not stay long and I shall run the business while he's gone. God and the devil will keep my good luck right with you while Ed is away. I can't stand it but the best thing to do I suppose is to endure it. But that is getting very monotonous. I know. I have not drunk a drop since last I saw you and the boys don't know what to make of it. Oily Gammons looks at me as if I was off my nut and I guess [indecipherable]

Oily and his dame got thrown out of a buggy the other day but did not get hurt, has a wagon and a blacksmith bill to pay however. I guess he will pay it if money comes.

There was 27 car loads that went to the picnic this morning, principally tid bits and tid bit hunters. I expect they will have a good time. I might have went but my last picnic was enough. I expect next month will be a grand picnic for me it is hard to tell yet. I send you the china [money.]

Bill and Fred make a fine team. I wonder where they got their money, from someone else I guess. Be good. Regards to Emma. Good luck.

all my love,
Emi

Marks must have something to do with a mine now. He has obtained some ore and has had a friend mill it.

To mill ore, it must first be pulverized. It is then mixed with water and various chemicals in a large round pan which spins at high speed. The pan is much like a kitchen mixer and does just about the same job. Mercury is added, causing the silver to amalgamate.

It seems, while Marks' ore was being milled, a rock caused one of the pans to break, a freak accident. This has caused he and his friend to lose $200.

Ed and Marks are running some kind of business, it may have been a saloon. Marks would later run a saloon in Bodie.

One of the most popular summer pastimes for Virginia City people, were the picnics at Farmer Treadways in Carson City.

Farmer Treadway owned a large park with many trees, lush grass and a dance hall. The greenery was a welcome sight for Virginia City people as there was little of it in that mining camp.

On these picnics, there were special trains at cut prices which took carloads of people down to Carson. On this one particular day, Marks says there were 27 carloads.

July 30, 1879
Gold Hill

Dear Rosa,

your very short and cross letter is at hand today. I suppose you should write me in that strain. My neglect of you, or more properly speaking, your letters, was not caused by an attention to anybody else or by putting my time against anyone else but by business I was attending to for Ed. But as he returned I am once again able to answer your letters as before. It seems strange to me that you of all others should write as you do but I suppose you believe what you write, therefore you do so because you think it is true and right that you should do so.

I'm very sorry that I cannot do as you requested. But the china [money] and another small package was in the post office before I read your letter so I hope you will overlook it if it is wrong. It seems so strange that my bad luck should come between you and I. It makes me feel bad that you would believe that I don't think of you as I always did. You can think as you please for it is a privilege we all have and I shall do the same, I shall not quarrel.

O pardon the crowds awhile
I waste one thought I owe to thee
And self-condemned appear to smile
Unfaithful to thy memory

Nor deem that memory less dear
That then I seem not to repine
I would not fools should hear
One sigh that I should wholly be thine

I have got 2 blisters and it is doing me no good to write as I do. I am very, very hurt to see you wrote good-bye. I hope you don't mean it. I said nothing to you when you went to the **dinner party** and did not write me for days. I don't suppose all my writing will mend the matter or get me forgiven. My regards to Em. Love and kisses to yourself and believe as everyone
Erni

Rosa is again hurt because Ernest has not written her soon enough. She feels someone else is receiving his attention. In an effort to make him react in some way, she writes and breaks off with him. The ploy works. Ernest quickly writes back and attempts to reassure Rosa that he does care for her.

Marks again blames his troubles on his bad luck.

The lines of poetry are Marks'.

August 12, 1879, Rosa May returned to Virginia City. She was back at Cad Thompson's at 18 South D Street. The following letter was written by Rosa's friend, Emma, a Carson City prostitute.

Carson
Aug 15th 1879

Little friend Rosa,

Your letter was received yesterday. I was very glad to hear from you. I am pleased to hear that you are doing well. It must be an agreeable change to go out at night and come in the morning with a shining $20 more than you would see here in monthy. [I believe she means, "in a month's time."] I am sure your room looks very nice a splendid place for your **dear little Johnny** [customer] to slip in when he comes to see you. The dreamy waltz for instance. Phil has stopped cooking and Lilly and myself eat at the restaurant and have a pretty good time. I have not drawn a sober breath since I have been home. I also received from San Jose [a letter] When I saw the post mark it kind of sobered me. I thought it was from home but it was from some fellow by the name of Spencer. Leilly [Lilly] and Wilson was at the train to meet me and I saw your dear Johnny, my Billy and Mr.Brooks was here to see me Tuesday night, but he did not stay. They asked after you and told me to send their love to you when I wrote. Lilly was telling me that Mrs. Phillips said if you conderscended to bid her good by she would have opened a bottle of wine, ho, ho. Tell Miss Cad Thompson that I went to see about her stockings. They did not have any at present but they sent for them and they will be here as soon as they get them. My bird sings very sweet in the morning but not a word from him in the afternoon his voice is very weak. My Charley sends his love to you. Also Lilly and her Charley, I and also Emana Boyd. Give my love to Miss Cadd and remember me kindly to all the other girls. Answer soon.

> Yours Respectfully
> Emma

P.S. I saw Bell Graham she sends her love to and she says we will go up and see you soon.
> Emma

This interesting and informative letter was written by Emma Hall, later, Emma Goldsmith. Emma Hall was jailed in June,

1880 in Virginia City for theft. She was 27. She was an alcoholic and would eventually drink herself to death.

We do not know exactly what has caused Rosa's move back to Virginia City. She may have wanted a change, or be closer to Ernest, perhaps to make better money at Cad Thompson's. Business for the Carson prostitutes was not booming. "Its as quiet here as ever," Emma says.

Rosa has gone out at night and made $20, a miner's week wages. One would assume that Rosa was street walking in order to implement whatever she was making at Cad Thompson's. From this letter, it seems that Rosa was a boarder at Thompson's paying rent for a room, yet still free to work the streets.

Rosa was a tidy person and took great pleasure in her surroundings. She explains to Emma that her room is looking nice, "A splendid place for your **dear little Johnny.**" A "John," was a prostitute's customer.

Emma was from San Jose, California. She feared that the letter with the San Jose postmark was from her family. Prostitutes were often afraid their families would find them out.

Mr. Brooks, a customer of Emma's, was a successful Carson merchant.

Mrs. Mary Ann Phillips, then 58, was a Carson City madam who Rosa has most recently worked for. "...if you had condescended to bid her good-by, she would have opened a bottle of wine," seems to imply that Rosa was very prideful and may not have left Phillips' place on the best of terms.

Mining camp prostitutes were fond of birds, especially canaries. Ernest has mentioned Rosa's bird in several letters. Emma mentions her own. The custom of mining camp prostitutes owning birds, very likely came from the miner's use of canaries to detect bad air and smoke.

Emma's Charley, was Charles Young, and listed himself as, lover, in the Virginia City 1880 Census. He was 45, and lived on South D Street. Emana Boyd was a Carson City prostitute. Rosa is one among a number of girls working at Cad Thompson's.

Virginia City
Aug. 18th 1879

Friend Leo,

Having arrived in town again I write to inform you of my address and if you wish to call and see me I would be pleased to have you do so I am living with Mrs. C. Thompson.

Hoping to see you soon.
I am as ever
Yours Respectfully
Rosa May
No. 18 D St

This is the only sample of Rosa's handwriting. The note was a business letter to Leo Miller, a Virginia City jeweler and a good customer.

(No date)

Miss Rosa

Please come to my room to night if you wish come between 9 and 10. The front door will be open so walk right in to my room and I will be on up as soon as I close the store.

Isaac Isaacs

You know where I live?

Isaac Isaacs ran a clothing store at 38 South C Street in Virginia City with a man called Cohn. Evidently, Rosa sometimes operated as a call girl. Isaacs lived at a boarding house at 31 North C Street, ran by Mrs. Leconey. The boarding house was in a brick building above McMillan's and Adams' store.

The last letter from Ernest Marks:

Happy New Year
Virginia City
January 1, 1879 [he meant 1880]

My Own Rosa
        I am in receipt of both your letters. Oh! no my darling,
do not for a moment think your constant writing anoys me.
God bless you if it was not for those letters I don't know what
I should do now that I have you not in person to love, to talk
to. I forgive you darling for thinking that your dear letters
disturb me. I got your powder last night at Coles [a drug
store] and I hope to bring it tomorrow or the next day I
expect it will be just my luck to meet Reynolds but I shall go
in and brave it— I am making calls. I enclose you my card
and I am wishing it might be as last year that I might present
it in person   Tom is in a great hurry stop [Indecipherable] It
is rather a nice day   I see many callers out   I shall write you
a longer letter tomorrow   Just think my love, I have not
drank a drop today I know you will be glad to hear I am so
good Remember me to Em   Tom also   Oily Gammon
says happy new year to Rosa
        I do to and many returns — May my darling always be
happy— Sweet Kisses lots of prosperity for 1880
                                        Yours always
                                        Emi

        Five months since our last word, Rosa is back in Carson City.
Rosa was a constant letter writer and fears that this disturbs Marks.
Marks fears he will run into Tom Reynolds when he visits Rosa.
Marks again on the wagon.
        The following is the last letter, and an interesting one to end
with. It is from Cad Thompson, and addressed to Rosa at
Thompson's brothel in Virginia City.

San Francisco
March 27th, 1880

Friend Rosa,

I received your letter and was glad to hear from you. I am still crippled up with rhuematism and have not been out to see a woman Lena Beck and that Emma and Lily from Carson called to see me last night. Emma looks horrible and from her report of the mountains [business in Virginia City] I guess it will be hard work to get anyone to go there. The weather has been rainy, cold, and disagreeable ever since I came down [from Virginia City.]

Tell the Spanish woman to keep her house I don't want it, for if there is nothing in Virginia [no business in Virgina City] I will move my furniture down here as everyone seems to live in this place. I will try and get some women next week and run the house one trip and tell George that he need not mind whitening it until I see what we are going to do. I don't know why in hell Welch did not tell me what he wanted, Crittons or what he wanted and I would have sent it the same time I sent the other stuff. I am sorry you have been sick, I don't wonder, that damp, dreary house would make any body sick, it makes me sick to think that I have got to go back to it. Give Harry's and my kind regards to George. Hoping this finds you well and to hear from you soon. I remain yours respectfully. Mrs. C Thompson

By March 27, 1880, three months since the last letter, Rosa is again in Virginia City at Cad Thompson's brothel at 18 South D Street.

Thompson is now in San Francisco with Harry, her man. She may have gone to San Francisco to give her rheumatism a rest. Virginia City's cold winters drove many rheumatoid sufferers to San Francisco.

Emma, Rosa's good friend, and Lilly are in San Francisco.

Emma is looking terrible from her drinking.

I don't know who Welch or Crittons were.

Rosa has been sick again. "...I don't wonder, that damp, dreary house would make any body sick, it makes me sick to think that I have got to go back to it." Such a picture of Thompson's brothel is a far cry from the crystal chandelier, velvet curtains and flowing champagne we might otherwise imagine her place to have been. Thompson herself is not stable enough financially to remain in San Francisco. She is tied to her place in Virginia City, though it is not doing well. "I have got to go back to it," she says.

George was probably the house bouncer and handyman.

It seems that Thompson, a stickler for details, considers Rosa one of the more responsible girls and has left her place in her charge.

From this letter, one would think that Thompson would soon move to San Francisco. Times were getting harder in Virginia City for the prostitutes and madams. There was less money circulating and it was tough to get new girls to work in Virginia City. San Francisco seemed the place to be.

But Cad Thompson did not leave Virginia City in 1880. She stayed on. She was involved in two civil court matters in 1883. On June 6, 1885, the Virginia Chronicle carried these lines about her:

While sitting at the second-story window of her establishment on D street, last Saturday evening, the widow Thompson observed a young man whom she recognized as the 'Barbary Coast masher,' [pimp] holding a rope behind him and trying to coax her dog away, which was sitting in the doorway. Arming herself with a large bucketful of slops, she waited until the masher grasped the dog by the collar, when she emptied the entire contents of the bucket on his person. Adonis let go his hold and lit out in the direction of the north pole, closely followed by the affronted dog and at least half a dozen fleet footed female denizens of the Thompson 'mayzong,' armed with mops and stove pokers.

Cad Thompson, a woman of 53 in 1880, had operated brothels in Virginia City since the 1860's. She is mentioned three times in **The Journals of Alfred Doten.** Alfred Doten was owner and editor of the Gold Hill News, but lost the newspaper in 1878 as the Comstock declined. As a newspaperman, it was Doten's job to know the people and the doings on the Comstock. His daily journal, which covers a period of fifty-four years, is one of the most informative and accurate accounts of life on the Comstock. On November 18, 1866, Doten wrote:

Some fellows took No. 1's engine about 4 o'clock this morning and washed out old Cad Thompson's whore house— gave her hell— created quite a consternation among the law and order portion of the community— not the end of it yet— We shall have to see who rules the city now the rough or the decent men.

December 31, 1866, Doten notes that Thompson's place was known as "The Brick," which at this time was located on North D Street.

The property on North D Street, known as 56 N. D Street (1878-79 City Directory) was sold by Thompson May 27, 1892 to Jacob Tucker for $20. The lot is listed as lot 5 of block 66. This was directly across from the V and T freight depot. The lot is empty today, but nearby a large cottonwood grows.

I believe that this property was the site of Cad Thompson's first, and last brothel. The selling of the property in 1892 might have forced Rosa May to move elsewhere.

July 4, 1867, Doten writes that John Dolton resisted arrest in Cad Thompson's and was shot and killed by Hawkins, a policeman. Only hours earlier, Zink Barnes was accidentally shot by Hugh Kerrin, fire Chief, at the same place.

Throughout the 1870's, Cad Thompson appears on the lists of uncalled for letters and on the arrival and departure lists from

Virginia City. Now and then she was arrested for drunk and disorderly conduct.

The February 17, 1875 issue of the Territorial Enterprise, reveals that Thompson's real name was Sarah Hagan. Hagan was taken to court by Andrew Allison in an effort to repossess his house in the red light. What the circumstances were are not clear. Hagan fought Allison bitterly for about a month but lost the case.

Rosa May, about 1879. She was twenty-four. Courtesy Helen Evans.

Bodie Museum photo supposedly of Rosa May. Actually this is Laura
Davenport, prostitute friend of Rosa's. Courtesy Anthony Knapp.

Virginia City, Nevada in its glory. Arrow points to area on North D Street where Cad Thompson's "Brick house" brothel stood.

Virginia City about 1879. Carlton Watkins photo courtesy of California State Library.

Virginia City looking down from Sun Mountain. Nevada State Historical Society.

D Street Virginia City around 1930. Small buildings at right edge are the camp's last cribs.

(TOP) The only crib left today in Virginia City. Notice stairs leading down from saloon. Photo by author

(BOTTOM) D Street today. Virginia and Truckee freight depot on the left. Cad Thompson's "Brick house" was across the street near trees.

Carson City about 1880 looking southeast from Capitol. Two story is the Ormsby House at Carson and Second Streets. Arrow points to Ormsby Street and Carson red light district.

(TOP) Corner of Third and Ormsby (Curry). Jennie Moore's brothel stood here among other houses of prostitution.

(BOTTOM) Grave of Mary Ann Phillips in Carson's Lone Mountain Cemetery. Phillips was a madam mentioned in Rosa May's letters.

(LEFT) Mary Ann Phillips' house in Virginia City, a residence.

(BOTTOM) Two houses in Carson City once houses of prostitution.

(TOP) Louis Serventi's marker made around 1965.

(BOTTOM) The sign that supposedly marked Rosa's grave about 1961.
Courtesy Will P. Ralph.

Burton Frasher's 1927 photo of the Bodie cemetery showing Rosa's picket fence. Courtesy Burton Frasher, Jr.

Close-up of Rosa's fence, 1927. Courtesy Burton Frasher, Jr.

Bodie about 1900. Arrow points to Rosa's house in the red light. Photo by A.A. Forbes.

Bodie about 1900. Men hauling equipment for use in cyanide plant. Arrow points to Rosa's house. Courtesy Anthony Knapp.

Empty field where Rosa's house stood. My wife (arrow) stands at site of Rosa's house. Bodie jail to the left.

Looking up King Street toward old Chinatown. Jail is second building.

Bodie, 1927. Arrow points to Marks' saloon. Burton Frasher, Jr.

The letter that unlocked Rosa's story. Courtesy Helen Evans. Photo by Ron Brewer.

This could have been the scene as they dragged Rosa's coffin out of town to be buried in the winter of 1911-12.

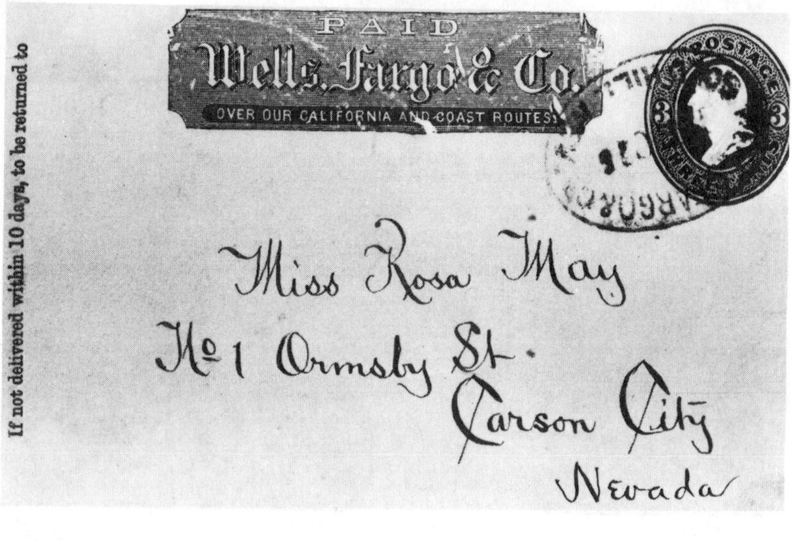
If not delivered within 10 days, to be returned to
PAID
Wells, Fargo & Co.
OVER OUR CALIFORNIA AND COAST ROUTES
Miss Rosa May
No 1 Ormsby St.
Carson City
Nevada

(TOP) The author replacing Rosa's picket fence in the Bodie outcast cemetery.

(BOTTOM) One of Rosa's envelopes. A gift from Helen Evans.

Hugh McCaghren }
To } Deed
Rosa May }

This Indenture made the 14th day of June
in the year of our Lord one thousand nine hundred & two
Between Hugh McCaghren of the City & County of San
Francisco State of California the party of the first part &
Rosa May of Bodie Mono County State of California the
party of the second part. Witnesseth. That the said party
of the first part for & in consideration of the sum of One
hundred & seventy five $175.00 Dollars lawful money of the
United States of America to him in hand paid by the said
party of the second part the receipt whereof is hereby acknowledged
does by these presents remise release & forever Quitclaim unto
the said party of the second part & to her heirs & assigns
all that certain lot piece or parcel of land situate in the
town of Bodie County of Mono State of California & bounded
& particularly described as follows to wit. That certain
lot no 42 in Block no 26 west side of Bonanza Street
as the same appear on the official map of the town of Bodie
Cal made by Leo A Scovell in 1880. Together with the
dwelling house & all improvements situate & erected on
said Lot no 42 Block no 26 aforesaid & whatever furniture
& fixtures belonging to & contained therein which said
dwelling house & improvements have been occupied by the
party of the second part upwards of 10 years as a residence
in said Bodie Cala

Together with all & singular the tenements hereditaments
& appurtenances thereunto belonging or in any wise appertaining
& the reversion & reversions remainder & remainders rents

Deed to Rosa May's house.

Rosa's red light, Bodie Museum. Photo by Rick Lancaster. Courtesy Gary Howard

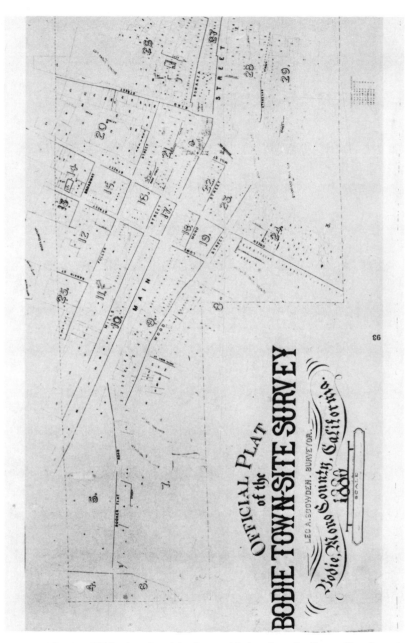

Map of Bodie, 1880, showing blocks and lots, given to the author by an anonymous enthusiast.

Chapter 10

Sitting in Helen Evans' living room, reading Rosa's letters for the first time, I knew little of what I've shared. True, the letters were a window through which I could peek at a few years of Rosa's life. But the window was fogged by the ornate Victorian script which made reading difficult; fogged by unfamiliar expressions, unknown identities and strange subtleties.

Five months of reserach had quickly passed. What had first seemed an easy task had become a mountain. My work was only beginning.

Hundreds of research hours would be required to decipher the letters. Persons mentioned had to be identified; unfamiliar expressions, defined. Virginia City, Carson City and the entire Comstock Lode had to be thoroughly studied. The era would have to be understood to place the letters in context. A thorough knowledge of early California and Nevada history was imperative.

The letters were a key to Rosa's life. But only deligent, time consuming research could provide the missing information needed to establish an accurate portrait of Rosa's life.

Overwhelmed by the amount of work that lay ahead, I gathered pennies and camping gear and headed back to Bodie. There, I hoped to recharge my enthusiasm. Perhaps Bodie could shortcut my work in some way.

As I sped down from Dead Man's Summit, Mono Lake stretched wide and blue. Beyond were the Bodie Hills. Dotted with pinon pines and sagebrush, the Hills lay green against the cold, autumn sky. The sun did not shine as brightly as it had during summer. A hard wind down from the mountains buffeted my VW.

Creeping over Cottonwood Canyon road, the wild, pungent smell of white sagebrush penetrated into the car. I loved the smell of sagebrush and I had missed it. Its fragrance seemed to contain every Western boom town that ever was and every gambler, gunslinger and whore that ever walked a sawdust-floored saloon.

Bodie lay like a silent ruin in the narrow, green valley. The cold had driven everyone but the park rangers away.

Hands in my pockets, jacket snug around my neck, head down, I walked Bodie's deserted streets alone. I crept around the brown weathered buildings, walked the back lots of trash and deserted wagons, climbed the hill to Rosa's grave. There, as usual, I paused, hoping for an inspired insight. None came.

I walked down from the cemetery, across town, past the silent Standard Mill, to Chinatown where Rosa lived and died. The field was empty of summer tourists. Even the cattle were gone, taken from the mountains at summer's end. At one end of the field, the jail sat quietly missing its once rowdy prisoners. A brick building lay crumpled in the middle of the field. A square of stones that once supported Rosa's house— the Palace it had been called during boom years; the stones lay like white, ancient bones. An icy wind came hard against my face. I walked back to my car through the wind. I was distressed. Bodie, the ghost town, with its eerie silence, could not give answers. I was resigned. If Rosa's story could ever be found, it would be found in courthouse files and faded newspapers; in ancient letters and memories of old timers.

Helen Evans had permitted me to reproduce her photograph of Rosa May. The 8 x 10 photograph stood in its frame on my writing desk. Rosa's sensitive eyes stared from the photograph twenty-four hours a day. Sometimes I stared back. A strong intuitive feeling had convinced me that there was a more meaningful story to be found in Rosa May's legend. At times I continued to feel the presence of something or somebody trying with great energy to push me forward, to open my eyes.

Days continued to be spent writing old-timers who had lived in Bodie. I reread Rosa's letters countless times and made notes.

There were always books to read, articles to check. Slowly, bit by bit, pieces were being laid in place.

Over the next two and a half years my enthusiasm held up. I uncovered information in seven major ways:

1. Newspapers of the era brought Rosa's time to life. These newpapers included the Virginia City, **Territorial Enterprise,** the **Gold Hill News, Carson Morning Appeal, Bridgeport Chronicle-Union** and the **Bodie Miner.** Fortunately, these newspapers had been preserved and were now on micro-film at the Nevada State Library in Carson City. I obtained them through inter-library loans. It was thrilling to find Rosa's name on the arrival/departure lists in Virginia City. Persons mentioned in the letters also turned up. With each newspaper, Rosa's time, her people and her town's became more real. I came to know the merchants who sold to her, the policemen she avoided, the miners, pimps, whores and madams she brushed arms with long ago.

2. Pacific Coast Directories and city directories helped to identify those mentioned in the letters.

3. Courthouse records in Bridgeport, Carson and Virginia City continued providing information.

4. State and Federal records, such as the 1875 Nevada Census and the 1870, 1880 and 1900 Federal Census helped to identify many. Passport records in Washington were also searched.

5. I managed to find more old-timers who had lived in Bodie while Rosa was alive. I drove to their cities and interviewed them. Each offered valuable bits of information.

6. Research reading covered California and Nevada history, with special attention given to Bodie, Carson and Virginia City.

7. Research of the history and causes of prostitution continued. Reading included books and articles by psychologists, sociologists, historians, prostitutes, pimps and madams.

Case studies by psychologists depicted the neglect and rejection prostitutes had experienced as young girls growing up in unstable homes. In most instances, girls had become prostitutes not because they were oversexed or desired money, but because of damaging relationships with parents. Prostitution for these women was really a complicated means of revenge and self-destruction.

I sympathized with prostitutes and the stories they told of their miserable home lives. From my own experiences, I was aware of the lack of self-esteem and the loneliness caused by troubled family relationships. And I was aware of the courage it took and the pain it caused to embrace the monster of one's past, to fight the fight one had to if one was to survive.

During research I found several books which clearly portray the prostitute's life and problems. In the following pages, Nell Kimball tells of her life as a parlour house prostitute and madam. Polly Adler, New York madam of the 1920's, 30's, and 40's discusses the girls who worked for her. And Harold Greenwald, psychoanalyst, summarizes his findings from interviews with twenty call girls. The following words will help you to better understand Rosa's life.

Chapter 11

Nell Kimball was born on a Missouri farm in 1854. (Rosa May was born in 1855.) Her large family was poor and her religious father was hard and mean. To escape the hopelessness of her home life, at fifteen she ran away to St. Louis with a Civil War veteran. The veteran soon deserted Kimball, who was thrown into the street with no money and no where to turn. She was determined, however, not to return to her family.

Eventually, Kimball was hired at Zig's, a high class parlour house. She remained a parlour house prostitute for the next ten years. Of these years, Kimball confesses she was a confused young whore who trusted no one and wanted nothing to do with love. In later years she realized she had wasted her youth.

At twenty-five she left prostitution to marry a bank robber. Her husband was killed two years later during a robbery. Kimball found herself a widow with a child. She did not want to go back to prostitution and was forced to work at carnival booths and factories for terribly low wages. She explains that working women were not respected.

Living alone, working for several years at low paying jobs, trying to make ends meet, to stay straight; Kimball neared emotional exhaustion. It was then that the final heart breaking blow came: her son died.

Deeply embittered by the deaths of her husband and child, Kimball contemplated suicide, but was determined to live. She returned to Zig's parlour house in St. Louis. There she met a wealthy tobacco capitalist. She was kept by this man for several years until the wife found out. Kimball was forced to flee St. Louis, but left with a healthy sum, enough to set up her own house.

She moved to New Orleans and searched Storyville for a suitable house. During the 1890's, Storyville was declared the New Orleans official red light district by city authorities in order to keep prostitution confined to one area.

Kimball found a two story house, filled it with fine furniture; bought beds and linen; hired maid, bouncer, and five or six beauties; paid off the local officials, and opened a high class, $20 parlour house which catered to successful professional men. She remained a madam for nearly forty years until November 17, 1917, when Storyville was officially closed by the Federal Government.

Kimball explains, that there was never a shortage of willing girls who wanted to become prostitutes. Most of these girls had landed in the city with no money, no job, no place to stay, much like Kimball herself at fifteen. She had little difficulty convincing them of the advantage of a square meal and a place to sleep.

Kimball blamed society for driving young girls into prostitution by not paying them enough for their labors. Masters and Benjamin, authors of **Prostitution and Morality,** elaborate the poor girl's predicament in the 19th century:

"....it was well established that a large proportion of all prostitutes then came from the ranks of the domestic servants — in England and on the Continent, as well as in the United States. Prostitution and the domestic service (along, sometimes, with sweat-shop labor) were almost the only careers open to an unmarried girl of the lower classes, and the near starvation wages paid to servants, in combination with long working hours, grueling toil, and frequently, cruel treatment, would have made prostitution the obvious career choice for most of such women had prostitution been less harshly condemned by the society. As it was, many women preferred censure to a thankless and ill-paid servitude."

With the coming of the machine age, society was changing from agricultural to industrial based. With the improvements in machines, factories were built. Many employed in factories were men and women who had left the struggles of farm life hoping city life and factory work would free them from their drudgery. But without labor unions and organization, laborers lacked the political clout which could force companies to pay fair wages. Both men and women were left at the mercy of powerful companies content to pay their employees pauper's wages. Still, a women received far less than a man for doing the same job for the same hours.

There was a reason for this.

During the 19th century, the man was the family provider. It was an offense to his pride, if his wife sought outside work in order to help support the family. It was a woman's duty to bear and care for children and handle domestic chores. It was man's sole duty to provide.

It was, therefore; a man's world and working women were a threat to his esteem and pride. It followed, that a man's labors were worth more and he was paid better.

The single woman and widow found themselves in a strange plight. Without men to provide support, they were unable to compete in the male centered society. Naturally, this made the easy wages of prostitution attractive.

In addition to the economic pressures, there were other moral restraints placed upon both men and women that increased the need for prostitutes in the 19th century.

Queen Victoria and Prince Albert had a profound influence upon the thinking of men and women in England, as in Europe and the United States. Queen Victoria has often been blamed for the austere morality of her reign. But it was her husband, Prince Albert, who actually advocated the idealistic and demanding morality which has become synonymous with the Victorian Era.

Victoria and Albert encouraged all men and women to live good wholesome lives, to strive for perfection, to try always to fulfill the Golden Rule. This led to the creation of a large number of worthy social causes: orphanages, hospitals, and labor unions which helped to achieve better wages.

But such an austere morality had a very negative effect on sexual attitudes. Sex became regarded as a necessary physical act whose sole purpose was creating children. Sexual drives and feelings were considered the lust of the flesh and were to be repressed — even in marriage. Few married men ever saw their wives entirely naked.

Because of the unnatural sexual repression of the Victorian Era, men, having more freedom in society, began to seek out women with whom they could release their pent up sexual frustration. Since sexual passions were considered base and sinful, and not to be consummated with the, "Good" woman — the future wife or mother — this led to a demand for a lower type of woman, the prostitute.

Prostitution, therefore; fulfilled certain needs for both Victorian men and women. For the Victorian male, it offered relief from sexual tensions. For thousands of poor women, it provided a means by which they could earn a living and achieve the material and creature comforts they otherwise would have been denied.

But prostitution was naturally an awful blemish in the highly moral Victorian society. Its presence could not be ignored by decent men and women, especially when girls as young as ten or eleven were involved.

With the spread of prostitution, there arose numbers of social reformers who attempted to deal with the problem. Some reformers were religious people simply outraged by the increase in public prostitutes. Other reformers were deeply troubled by the way poor women were forced to live, destroying their bodies and spirits in the process.

All reformers, regardless of religious, moral or humane concern, fell into two factions: 1) the Abolitionist, who sought to completely abolish prostitution from society, and 2) the Regulationist, who believed prostitution was inevitable, the best course being the lawful regulation of prostitution in order to check disease, thereby protecting innocent women and children. Regulationists were far more realistic in dealing with the awesome problem. They were in favor of licensing prostitutes and in setting up clinics where prostitutes could be examined and treated for disease. Abolitionists were appalled by this, for they believed the regulation of prostitution meant the acceptance of the social evil and would have no part of this.

Regulationists and Abolitionists could not reconcile their differences and fought bitterly from 1860 until 1917, when wide open prostitution was outlawed in most cities. As a result of their irreconciliation, prostitution continued unregulated, causing widespread disease and the physical, emotional and spiritual destruction of thousands of young girls and women.

Victorian reformers wasted time and energy in efforts to eradicate and regulate prostitution. Their energies would have been better spent aiding their society to come to grips with the major causes of prostitution: 1) low wages for poor working women and, 2) the unhealthy sexual repression of the Victorian Era. It is an irony how the banterings among reformers and resulting newspaper publicity, brought prostitution ever more into the public's attention, causing terrific stimulation for the skin trade.

The boom in prostitution brought more adamant pleas from the clergy and certain reformers for the reformation of man's "wicked ways." This led to the formation of the fanatical Purity Movement, 1885-1900, bent on the moral betterment of man, to be achieved by the internalizing and discipline to certain prescribed moral values. The Purity Movement, merely urged stricter self-control of sexual passions. It further increased sexual guilt and drove men to prostitutes in their attempts to rid themselves of their guilt and sexual frustrations.

Victorians never accepted the idea, that God created sexual desires to insure the propagation of the human being.

All of this had a profound influence on Nell Kimball as a 19th century woman, prostitute and madam. For her animosity with her society and hatred of its hypocrisy were feelings that were developed through experience.

Kimball's negative experiences with her society's conflicting values began with her father, who preached love and mercy but was without feeling for his wife and children. It was from him that Kimball learned to distrust religion and the social values religion advocates. Her father's unkindness left Kimball with an emotional scar that never healed.

Her budding bitterness and anger were reinforced as a fifteen year old prostitute servicing the sexual needs of successful professional men with wives and families at home. Seeing society's best at their worst, made Kimball aware of society's hypocrisy.

Her bitterness was further nurtured as a young widow, as she struggled to go straight, while working for pauper's wages, barely able to support herself and her child.

Finally; as madam for many years, forced to pay off city bureaucrats, police and wealthy landlords — Kimball was convinced of society's hypocrisy and greed.

There was, therefore; a great bond among fellow prostitutes and madams. For they saw themselves as victims of society's hypocrisy and lack of genuine concern, women who were used sexually and profited from economically. Women upon whom were thrusted society's lonely and unloved; violent and frustrated; women who were adored until coitus. They were society's scapegoat, someone to pitch stones at when that society could not admit it was unable to deal honestly and maturely with sex, nor accept responsibility for the poor wages that were driving women into prostitution.

Though poor wages made prostitution attractive, Kimball herself admits, there there were still other reasons girls became prostitutes.

Some girls were simply foolish and had no idea of what they were getting themselves into. Many were once singers, dancers and entertainers who really didn't have much talent. Many of these fooled themselves. As soon as they made enough to buy new music and new costumes, they'd get out of the racket. Most never did nor admitted they were full time whores.

There were smart girls who liked the isolation and protection as a parlour house prostitute. Kimball explains, that such women were generally unhappy and afraid of the outside world. And, they tended to drink more than other whores.

Others, liked the rebellious life style, the easy money, fancy clothes, fine food and liquor. But for most, prostitition was just another way of making a living, earning enough for food and clothing and a bit of luxury. Most were ordinary people doing a job society would not admit there was a need for. The only criterion for a good whore was a genuine desire to be one; a girl had to take pride in what she could offer a man.

Kimball ran a $20 house, $10 during depressions. Most houses usually opened at noon , and closed in the early morning. A girl could make between $50 and $200 a week. But most girls were always broke. (A common laborer at top pay, would have had to work ten weeks to make $200.) The girls spent their money on dressmakers, stockings, hats, perfume, ivory comb sets, jewels, things that weren't worth much when a girl had to pawn them.

A girl also threw a lot of money to her pimp, who often tried to get her hooked on drugs, mostly opium, in order to control her. The men these girls loved were the real trouble in their lives. The girls were often overly sentimental and easy to manipulate. They felt depressed if they didn't have a steady man. Most had lost any sexual feeling except for their pimp. Yet even on this debased level, women needed love and this need kept them human. For they often felt disgraced and looked down upon by their customers. There was a genuine desire, on the whore's part, to be respected as a human being. That they were not, made most prostitutes sad, and they turned to pimps for token love and occasional affection.

The occupational hazards and torment of the prostitute's life were insufferable. Consider one of her days:

She wakes in the early afternoon and comes downstairs for coffee. She never feels like eating much and the madam has to force her to eat breakfast.

She sits or lies about during the afternoon, plays cards, gossips with the other girls. Usually she has no interests and may begin to drink. Sometimes, she goes shopping, buys a new dress, hat, jewelry or perfume.

In the early evening, she dresses in a fine gown, but nothing too fancy. When the johns arrive, the madam calls her and five or six other girls downstairs. The johns may be repeat customers or strangers.

The girl goes into her act: she is sweet, she is pretty, she is dumb, she is willing, she has no needs, she is a servant, she'll do whatever any man wants.

She sits with the other girls beside their customers at the long mahogany dining table. The talk is gay, the other girls giggle, she giggles too. The men are buying and pouring champagne, $20 a bottle. The madam is charming, witty, strong, in control.

Dinner finished, the girls and johns move into the parlour. There is a bar where a brawny bouncer serves as bartender. The girls and johns sip drinks.

She is gay and cool as she makes her hustle. Finally, one of the men chooses her. She leads him up the stairs by the hand, one hand on the banister, to her room and the big bed. She does anything he wants her to do and says anything he wants her to say. If the john is a repeat customer, she knows his needs and goes about her business self-assured. This is one thing in life she knows she does well. She moans, but she is not aroused. It is all an act, but it is thoroughly convincing. As she goes through the motions, she hopes he will come soon so she can get on to the next customer. But she does not rush him, bad business, it would hurt his feelings and ruin his tip.

It's over. She washes the john down with hot water and soap. If he picks up anything, he'll know he didn't get it from her. She smiles and jokes as she washes. The john is drunk and feels relieved after the workout. She helps him dress. As he leaves he palms a gold coin on her dresser. She smiles and thanks him.

Immediately the girl begins to douche. There are several to choose from: lysol, bichloride of mercury, mercuric cyanide, carbolic acid and potassium permanganate. Afterwards, the girl dresses and combs her hair. The maid rushes in to change the sheets and makes the bed for the next john.

Meanwhile, the john has gone downstairs and the madam has graciously collected the $20, part of which belongs to the girl. The madam asks if he is pleased. He is.

The john either leaves but more often stays to visit with the other johns, many of whom he knows or does business with. The parlour house is sort of a social club, they meet here often, sometimes just to visit the girls and other men. Sometimes the men play poker, but the girls try to steer them away from gambling. They know men prefer gambling to screwing.

The girl comes downstairs and begins to hustle another customer. She may hustle as many as twenty or thirty a night and rarely will one arouse her.

She may work as late as five or six in the morning. Sometimes a john will stay the night. If none stay the night and work is over, she goes out with her pimp or with other girls to a restaurant. Over food and coffee, the girls discuss their various customers, especially the weird ones.

If the girl has a pimp, she'll hand over most of her night's earnings. If she has done well, the pimp will be pleased and will treat her kindly. If she hasn't done well, he may beat, scold, or deny her affection. She tries to do well so her pimp will be pleased and be nice to her. Her pimp is everything to her, her God, her master, her lover. As abnormal as it seems, her relationship with him is the most important human contact she has.

If the girl does not have a pimp, she's probably blue. All night, men have pawed and used her and not one has given a damn about her feelings. She may start to drink hard, snuff "snow" (cocaine) or take laudanum, a liquid preparation of opium, to ease the pain of her lonelinsess. If she goes low enough, she may kill herself, which is not uncommon. If not,

147

she'll return to the house, sleep until the next afternoon, waking to repeat the same routine that hardly ever changes. One day a week she is given off to spend with her pimp or go where she likes. She is like a little girl living at home under strict rules. Responsibility for her life is put in someone else's hands, at least temporarily.

Such was the whore's routine, years without thought, planning or meaning. It was a rare girl, who, after some years in the trade, lived a normal, happy life. Many were constantly depressed, eventually cracked up or killed themselves. Suicide was a haunting demon in every whorehouse.

The loneliness of a prostitute's life, even the high class parlour house girl, was immense. Cut off from her family by disgrace, the resulting shame and loneliness was awesome. She had placed herself in a world where she was used by everyone: by customers, madams, pimps, and often lesbian lovers.

To add to her troubles, there was the constant threat of pregnancy or disease, Little Casino (gonorrhea) or Big Casino (syphilis.) And there were always the crazies; over polite men who cracked their knuckles and beat or killed prostitutes whenever they had the chance.

The life was hard on a girl and wore her down physically, emotionally and spiritually. Unlike other professions, a prostitute's money making years were few. She started at top pay and her earnings decreased as her youth and beauty faded.

A girl, at best, lasted half a dozen years in a quality parlour house. After that, she usually became a street hooker, whispering arousing offers, exposing herself on street corners. The parlour house girl, who had been protected by the madam, well fed and clothed, and known the best customers, found street hustling terribly humiliating. As Dolly Fine, another madam, once said, "There is nothing more pitiful in life than a prostitute who has risen from the streets, tasted luxuries and liked them, and then finds herself once again in the gutter." Rather than live with the fall, many fading prostitutes chose suicide.

Polly Adler's autobiography, **A House Is Not A Home,** a best seller, provides further insight into the lives of prostitutes through the eyes of an intelligent, observant woman. Though a madam of more recent years, Polly Adler's comments often parallel those of Nell Kimball.

Polly Adler, like Kimball, had no trouble procuring girls. Quite the opposite, "...far from having to lure girls there, I was forced to turn away 30 or 40 for every one I was able to accommodate." There were many girls who knocked on her door who were not cut out for the hard life of prostitution. Adler persuaded many of them to go home.

The girls she did hire were experienced, willing and eager. She did not hire novices. All of her girls were pretty, had good health and were clean.

Most girls prostituted themselves for money. There were a few who did it for kicks, there were always a few extremists who loved whoring. At the other extreme were the girls who detested the life, girls, who gave their customers smiles while hating them. Adler admits, "For 99 out of 100 girls, going to bed with a customer," was, "a joyless, even distasteful experience."

Most of the girls were of average intelligence. None had any intention of staying in the business. Most were aware a career in prostitution was short lived and reserved for the young. The smart ones saved for retirment. But most weren't smart. They blew their money and used this as an excuse to stay in the life. Most made no preparation for the future. Some didn't know when to quit, others wouldn't try anything else.

Some were quite talented — actresses, dancers singers. They spent their days working at their craft. The majority, however; spent their time at the beauty parlour, at the movies or played cards, hearts their favorite. The reason they didn't do much in their off hours, Adler explains, was because of their strenuous work. After eight or ten hours of mental and physical exercise, they had no desire to exert themselves.

Adler:
    Inevitably I had a few lesbians, some of them troublemakers some very peaceful souls. It's often been said that a prostitute becomes so tired of being mauled by men that she turns to a woman for tenderness. Maybe so. I have no figures on the incidence, but it's my observation that it occurs in every walk of life.

And:
    I have said my girls were go-getters, but it wasn't only because of the money that they liked to keep busy. It was also an escape from thinking. Even the least introspective could not always avoid recognizing the precariousness of her position — and the loneliness of it. By becoming a prostitute, a girl cuts herself off not merely from her family, but from such a great part of life. She is isolated not just by social custom but by working conditions, and she has to some extent deprived herself of her rights as a citizen for which she has forfeited the protection of the law. It is not syphilis which is the occupational disease of the prostitute, but loneliness.

    Loneliness hit hardest at holidays, especially Christmas and New Year's. Many of the girls had sent their relatives gifts. By New Year's they were down in the dumps. They hadn't received so much as a thank you note.
    New Year's was the worst holiday because it was a time of planning for the new year. "Most prostitutes," Adler explains, "try to avoid thinking of the future and the passing time...Youth is their capital. For a whore, New Year's is a season of regret for the past rather than one of hope for the future."
    Adler thought a prostitute could count on no more than ten money making years. "Then she is through — if not dead or diseased, so broken by drugs, alcohol and the steady abuse of her body that no one will hire her again."
    All her girls were sentimental, and to escape their loneliness,

enjoyed going to clubs to hear crooners sing the sad ones. Many shed tears during torch songs for their love lives were often unhappy. Many had pimps who mistreated them. And Adler, like Kimball, had no great love for pimps:

I cannot deny that I mortally hate pimps. Still, in the long run, they are also victims — though not so obviously or so pitifully — along with the girls they exploit. Most of them come from poverty-stricken homes, and they acquire their education in the streets and in the pool halls, first out front, then in the back room. Their only talent seems to be that they have a way with women, and they find this out hanging around the dance hall chippies, the drugstore waitress and the high school sweater girls who flaunt their sex and ask for attention.

The pimp doesn't feel that he's doing wrong in putting his girls to work. He and the girls are in it together to trim the suckers. He thinks of himself as a smart operator, and sees nothing shameful in exploiting women and living on their earnings. (To his mind, all men exploit women to some degree.) He regards himself as an employer or a property owner, not as a criminal or a parasite. He considers that in taking over certain responsibilities for his girls, managing them, booking them into houses, getting them out of jail, teaching them the ropes, he earns the money the girls give him. He dins it into each girl that if she wants to survive she must give him unquestioning obedience. In return for the money she makes (which he teaches her she could not earn without him) he listens to her complaints and is kind to her, when he has the patience and when she has earned enough to safisfy him. Since these girls almost never find men who care for them — what man wants to love a prostitute? — their relationship with the pimp constitutes the only important human tie they have.

Just as the prostitute never, until the very end, is able to perceive that she is the victim, so the pimp never regards himself as exploited. He would be thunderstruck if it were pointed out to him that he has a miserable life, despised by other men, by madams he meets and deals with, by the underworld and by society. He thinks he is a very clever character, a sharp guy, able to make a buck and put up a front... the average pimp becomes an alcoholic and/or a drug addict, and in his last days a panhandler.

If prostitution was such an awful life, what drove girls into it in the first place?

Adler:
In my opinion the single factor— and the common denominator in an overwhelming majority of cases— is poverty. It is true that, though many girls are poor, only a small percentage of them take to hustling. But there is more than one kind of poverty— there is emotional poverty and intellectual poverty and poverty of the spirit. As well as material lacks, there can be a lack of love, a lack of education, a lack of hope. And out of such impoverishment the prostitute is bred.

In an effort to discover the major causes of prostitution, Harold Greenwald, a psychoanalyst, conducted intensive interviews with twenty call girls. His findings differed only slightly from Polly Adler's. Emotional impoverishment seemed to be the greatest cause of prositution today.

Of the twenty prostitutes Greenwald interviewed, not one came from a home where there a was a permanent, well adjusted marriage. Not one admitted growing up in a happy home where parents got along well. In seventy-five percent of the cases, homes were broken up by adolescence. In the remaining cases, the girls never saw any evidence of sympathy or affection between parents. Two girls had parents that went through three divorces; three girls from families where there were six divorces; and six girls saw their mothers living with men to whom they were not married. Because of the absence of warmth and permanence in their families, these girls had not been able to form an attachment to either parent, and hence; were not able to absorb the values of society which we most often learn from parents to whom we feel close.

The general attitude of such parents toward their children seemed to be one of complete rejection. The girls were rejected by fathers who didn't care about them, left home or died; and by mothers who never let them forget how much they had sacrificed for them. Nineteen of the twenty girls admitted feeling rejected by both parents.

In addition, many of the girls were thrown from one home to the next. Three girls were passed from family to family; three girls from one foster home to another; four lived in a succession of boarding schools.

It was from such a background of neglect and rejection that ten girls reputed engaging in early sexual activity for which they were rewarded. They learned early that they could barter sexual favors for affection, interest and attention. By providing sexual gratification, they were temporarily able to overcome their feelings of loneliness and unworthiness — while at the same time expressing their hostility toward parents for having neglected them.

Chapter 12

On the morning of June 1, 1900, Cecil Burkham, who ran Burkham's Dry Goods in Bodie and operated a stage between there and Hawthorne, Nevada; began walking each of Bodie's dirt streets, knocking on doors and asking questions. Burkham had been hired by the Federal Government to record the 1900 Federal Census of Bodie Township. It took Cecil Burkham sixteen days at fifty persons per day to record each of Bodie's eight hundred citizens.

On June 6, nearing the end of his rounds, he walked up King Street through Chinatown, went north at Bonanza Street, then down a slight incline. There were only three little white houses on Bonanza Street. He knocked on her door, feeling a bit embarassed to be doing so in plain daylight. A stout, dark haired woman, unaccustomed to daytime visitors, opened the door. She was tired and answered Cecil Burkham's questions quietly. Burkham carefully wrote her answers down near the bottom of his tally sheet. Name: Rosa May. Head of household. White female. Born January, 1855. Forty-five years old. Birthplace: Pennsylvania. Parents: Irish, born in Ireland. Embarassed, Burkham listed her occupation as seamstress, then a common misnomer for prostitute. She had been employed twelve months. She was able to read, write and speak English, and she rented her house. Burkham asked her if anyone lived with her. She lied. She said, no. Cecil Burkham thanked her and went to the two remaining houses on Bonanza Street. Chinamen lived in the two houses and Burkham wrote their answers down quickly. Finished with his quota, he shut the census docket and walked back to his store on Main Street for lunch.

On a blistering July day, nearly one year since I began my search, I drove down to the National Archives and Service Center at Laguna Niguel, California. There I found Rosa May listed in the 1900 Federal Census of Mono County, California. The census provided the first recorded information I had found regarding Rosa May and answered several important questions.

For one, the census proved that Rosa May was still alive June 6, 1900. This was a direct contradiction with Serventi's gravestone which claims she died in 1880. The fact that Rosa May had died after June 6, 1900, strengthened the possibility that people who had known Rosa May might still be alive.

Second, the census meant there were twenty fewer years in which records could have been destroyed, records located somewhere that might provide some insight into Rosa's life.

Third, the 1900 Census finally gave Rosa's obscure life a place and time of beginning: Pennsylvania; January, 1855. Unfortunately, the census did not specify the city or county of birth, information that would have certainly helped. However; knowing that Rosa was born in 1855, I was able to determine that between 1876-80, when Rosa May was living in Carson and Virginia City, she was between twenty-one and twenty-five years of age. In 1900, twenty years later, she was now forty-five and still prostituting.

Fourth, the census proved another portion of Ella Cain's story was untrue. Rosa May was not French and born in Paris. She was Irish, born of Irish immigrants somewhere in Pennsylvania.

Carefully studying the Bodie census, I found that on June 6, 1900, Rosa May was the only woman living in the Chinatown and red light area. Of the town's 800 men, women and children, there were 235 single men and but 50 single women including elderly widows. That meant five men for every single woman. Rosa May, being the only prostitute in town at the time, certainly had an overwhelming business.

The 1900 census also corroborated information I had discovered earlier. Richie Conway said he had delivered milk to Rosa May in 1902. There was now proof that Rosa May was alive in 1900, making Richie's recollection appear accurate. In addition, Sadie Cain, whom I had recently interviewed, said she saw Rosa May rocking on her porch about 1904-05. And Anna McKenzie, who I spoke of earlier, saw Rosa May between 1908-10. From this information, I now believed Rosa May could have lived as late as 1910, making her fifty-five at death.

Over the next several years, other facts would emerge. Early newspapers would help to identify the people and events of Rosa May's life. But the most important and revealing information would come from Rosa May herself. It would happen this way:

Mary Ann Phillips ran a house of prostitution on the southwest corner of 4th and Ormsby Streets in Carson City. She had bought the large two story place from Jennie Dupey for $3,350, December 5, 1874. That was quite a large sum in those days. A miner making top pay would have had to work for five years, saving every penny he made, in order to purchase the same house. Phillips, then fifty-three, a mother with a family, knew the house was a wise investment. The great silver bonanza had recently been discovered in Virginia City. A house in Carson City was ideal. Scores of men were employed at the Carson woodyards and silver mills. There was the State Legislature and the myriads of travelers who would pass through Carson on their way to Virginia City.

About five o'clock in the afternoon of August 12, 1879, twenty-four year old Rosa May left Phillips' place with her beat-up leather bags in hand. Her trunk would be sent later. Times were hard on the Carson girls now that Virginia City's mines were on the decline. More men were being laid off with each week. Rosa's stay at Mary Ann Phillips' house had not gone well. The girls had had to walk the streets in order to hustle up trade. Money was tight and times were not like they had been several years earlier when the men all had jobs. Feeling more money was to be made in Virginia City, Rosa was now on her way back.

At five o'clock, the sun still beat hard on Carson City. Rosa felt drops of perspiration trickle from her armpits and down her sides as she walked the ten blocks to the V and T depot at Carson and Washington streets. She dropped her bags every block or so in order to wipe the sweat from her forehead before the salty drops slid into her eyes.

At the V and T depot, she bought a ticket for two dollars and spent two hours on the train as it twisted back and forth up the mountain switch-backs to Virginia City. She smelled the burning pine wood through the train window all the way back to Virginia. The smell of burning pine was a familiar one and she liked the smell.

The train passed through Gold Hill, then over the Divide and into Virginia City. The depot was located at the corner of Union and D streets, in the middle of the red light district.

Rosa May walked a block from the depot to Cad Thompson's brothel at 18 South D Street, on the west side of D between Union and Taylor, about the middle of the block. Thompson's place was a wooden two story building which she rented though Thompson owned the "Brick" at 56 North D Street.

On the morning of August 18, 1879, Rosa May sat down at a desk at Cad Thompson's. She'd gotten up especially early in order to take care of some business before the other girls awoke and disturbed her. By mid-morning, Thompson's was already stifling hot. Rosa wiped beads of sweat from her forehead and thought of the money.

Taking a piece of baby-blue paper from the drawer, she dipped her quill into a small jar of dark blue ink. Rosa wrote a quick letter to Leo Miller, a jeweler and one of her best customers. She hoped Miller was still in town. She explained to him that she was back at Cad Thompson's and asked if he would visit her. She carefully addressed his letter and laid it beside the other letters, also being mailed to best customers.

Finished with her writing, Rosa bundled the letters together and walked up D Street to Union, then up the hill to C Street and mailed the letters at the Post Office. She walked back down to

Thompson's, smiling to herself, hoping her best customers would soon call.

Unfortunately, Leo Miller had left Virginia City. Several days later his letter was returned to Rosa, who, no doubt, was disappointed. But Rosa's disappointment would prove an invaluable asset in uncovering her story.

By an incredible stroke of fate, Leo Miller's letter would be mistakenly kept by Rosa among her love letters for more than thirty years. If Rosa had destroyed Miller's letter on its return, or if she had discarded the letter in the intervening years, not a trace of her handwriting would have survived. Rosa's story would have remained a secret. For it would be Rosa's own handwriting that would reveal the truth of her life: the reasons she had chosen prostitution, and the fact that she was indeed the self-sacrificing woman legend claimed.

A good friend, deeply interested in the Rosa May search, made me aware of the importance of Rosa's handwriting. My friend had studied graphoanalysis briefly and learned that handwriting analysis is able to reveal personality and motivations. She offered me several books on graphoanalysis which I took home, read and studied for several months.

I was at first skeptical of graphoanalysis. But I was willing to give the science a chance for the sake of whatever information it might reveal regarding Rosa May.

After several months of study, I began to apply what I had learned by doing brief graphoanalyses on my own of both friends and strangers. Using the basic elements of graphoanalysis, I was amazed by how much I could learn about a person simply through their handwriting. This sort of testing convinced me of the credibility of graphoanalysis. I then sought professional graphoanalysts.

Photographs of Rosa's handwriting were examined by professional graphoanalysts: Judy Craig, of Riverside, California; and Verna Lea Turner of Bakersfield, California. Both graphoanalysts agreed, that an absolutely thorough analysis of Rosa's personality was impossible based on the small amount of writing. Despite this obstacle, both graphoanalysts— miles apart and without knowledge of the other— reached similar conclusions regarding Rosa's life and personality.

In addition, the handwriting of Ernest Marks was also analyzed by Judy Craig.

Rosa May was twenty-four when she wrote Leo Miller in Virginia City. She was a pretty, bright-eyed, petite young woman, with soft, curly brown hair and fair skin. She was a woman, graphoanalysts assured, who took particular interest in her appearance. She would have dressed neatly at all times, taking extra special care with her hair, makeup, nails, etc. She was an attractive woman and would have drawn the attention of both men and women.

As a person, there was a lot to like about Rosa. She had a people winning personality— a real charmer, and no doubt used this talent to get what she wanted in life. She was very emotional and responded to people and situations immediately, without thought. She was quick to laugh at a joke and the first to shed tears when a sad story was told. She was irrepressible— very herself, most often friendly, talkative, with a wonderful sense of humor. She was thoughtful, took an interest in others, was warm and good hearted. She would have never intentionally harmed anyone.

She was frank and would tell the truth as she saw it. She was loyal, both to people and ideas. She generally did not run from problems, but was flexible and would adjust— and in the end, stubbornly resist. She carried herself with a certain stubborn pride and dignity. She might have been a whore, but people were going to respect her as a human being.

She was quite intelligent, logical, always making plans, but did not always rely on her good judgement. Her impulsiveness caused her to often do or say things without thinking.

She possessed a number of negative personality traits that impeded her life, and very likely were reasons which led her to prostitution. These qualities are often found in the personalities and backgrounds of the compulsive-neurotic prostitute.

Though Rosa seemed to others, a happy, well adjusted person, in control of her life; she was actually prone to great anxiety. Like many prostitutes, she lacked self-respect. She felt poorly about herself. This led Judy Craig to conclude, that very likely Rosa had an unhappy childhood. There was evidence that Rosa had been made to feel poorly about herself very early in life. Also, it was obvious, that she had grown up in an extremely strict home. Being an intelligent, free spirited woman, Rosa had resented the sternness and the moral principles that were shoved down her throat. She could think for herself and did not go along with her parent's ideas. There was evidence that they had demanded that she accept their ways and she had resisted this. Rosa had deeply resented their control.

Ironically, in her life as a prostitute, she had continued the pattern of being controlled by others. She was now controlled by pimps, madams, customer's needs and circumstances, yet; she longed terribly to be free.

Rosa's mother and father were Irish immigrants— likely farmers from southern Ireland. More than a million Irishmen fled Ireland during the potato famine 1845-50.

Ninety percent of Ireland was Catholic. This may help to explain the overly-strict home in which Rosa grew up. For Irish Catholicism, had been negatively influenced by Jansenist priests. Jansenists advocated a fanatical suppression of sexual feelings. Women, for instance, were told to bathe clothed in order to avoid the "mortal sin" of seeing their naked bodies. Such ideas created tremendous guilt in regards to normal sexual feelings.

Such Catholicism was generally overly harsh, and without compassion for human weaknesses, Jansenism being a religious left-over from the Middle Ages.

From her handwriting, it seems that Rosa was not allowed to challenge the harsh beliefs her mother and father upheld. No doubt, this lack of freedom eventually led Rosa to leave home— and in later years, helped to cause tremendous confusion in regards to morality.

Rosa's lack of self-respect, reflected in her self-consciousness and in her fear of criticism. For instance, though she was quite intelligent, and capable of making her own decisions, she was indecisive, afraid to say "yes" or "no" and mean it. She clearly lacked faith in her abilities and in her own mind. Without faith in herself, motivation was crippled. Circumstances or other people were going to make her decisions for her.

Compounding this, was her confusion in regards to morality. Rosa did not know what was right or wrong. There was little evidence in her handwriting that she possessed a code of ethics to guide her life. I had felt this myself while reading Marks' letters.

Combined with her lack of ethics, was a nature that was quite susceptible to temptations. She lacked self-control in some instances. Nor did Rosa care much about her integrity or reputation. Verna Lea Turner concluded — without my telling her— that Rosa May was immoral and likely a prostitute.

Rosa, then; at twenty-four, was living in a strange half-world, without laws or direction. Yet, she was desperately seeking someone or something to guide her life.

Lacking faith in herself, and a code of ethics to help her judge between right and wrong, Rosa could have easily been talked into conclusions by pressure or persuasion. Here was a confused young girl perfect prey for pimps and madams.

Judy Craig believed somewhere between Rosa's old life under her parents and her new life as a prostitute, something traumatic had happened. It may have been an unhappy home life that led to a bad marriage or bitter love affair. She may have been smooth talked into prostitution by a pimp or madam. Whatever, there was, Craig felt; a "link" missing between Rosa's former life and her present as a prostitute.

Rosa had willingly placed herself in a terribly hard world in which she could be exploited, beaten, robbed, murdered or generally abused. It was an extremely painful world and suicide was nothing new, a world in which no one could be trusted.

For Rosa, in a way, this world made perfect sense. Through her parents' lack of love she had learned that people betray. If one's parents couldn't be trusted, certainly no one could. She had merely continued the pattern she had learned as a child.

So, she was an extremely cautious woman for all her outward charm. She was quite selective with whom she became close. There were perhaps one or two she might have somewhat trusted. And of these, she was terribly jealous of their time and affections.

In general, she was distrustful and afraid of rejection. She kept people at bay, and because of this, was very lonely. The distance Rosa put between herself and others accounts for her living in Carson City much of the time, while Marks lived in Gold Hill, some twenty miles away.

Still, in her dealings with others, Rosa most often **acted** friendly, though she had a fault finding nature and allowed others to get on her nerves. At such times when she suspected imposition — and there were many — her bad temper would explode releasing a hoarde of cutting barbs. But her anger did not last long and her fits of temper were curbed by her tact, diplomacy and sense of humor.

A loner by nature, she coveted her privacy. Suspicious and distrustful, she needed more space than most people. Since she was so outgoing, there would be times when she needed to be alone simply to recover from emotional outlay. During such periods, she would feel emotional exhaustion, gloom, disgust, indifference — even despair. But she would recover once she had rested.

Though Rosa could have worked with others, she would have worked better with a small group — such as the usual brothel of five or six girls — or best by herself. Her fault finding, narrow-mindedness, and suspicious nature could at times make her difficult and bothersome to work with. This likely got her fired by madams — or drove customers away.

All in all, she was a simple woman and did not want a great deal from life, a roof over her head, food, a little affection, enough money to meet immediate needs. Like most prostitutes, she lived for the moment. She was sensitive, earthy and appreciated the little things that make life meaningful.

Her interests tended toward good books, good music, the theater, art, music, etc. She was dextrous and had artistic talent. She may have drawn, painted, did needle work or played a musical instrument. It is interesting to note, that in the winter of 1877, an R. May was going door to door in Virginia City selling prints of the works of Antonio Conova, a 19th century sculptor.

Rosa was an independent woman and enjoyed traveling. Considering her emotional problems, her lack of motivation, her charm — for Rosa, prostitution was an ideal life.

One more thing: Rosa May was easily tempted to share and help others, even at a sacrifice to herself. She could very easily have been the good hearted prostitute who died trying to save stricken miners, as the Bodie legend claims.

In 1879, Ernest Marks was twenty-four, about 5'7", medium build, dark complected, dark eyes, dark hair. He was a German-Jew and came with his family to America in 1866 when Marks was eleven. The family later settled in Gold Hill. He had at least one brother and one sister. His father was an alcoholic.

Ernest Marks was a real hell raiser, a domineering man with a vicious temper, capable of violence. He over-indulged himself in everything — drank too much, screwed too much, ate too much. When Judy Craig asked me how old Marks was, she was shocked when I told her, twenty-four. Here was a man, she said, whose health was that of a middle aged man who had spent his life abusing his body with too much drink and sex, whose nerves were totally shot. Decadent was the word for his life style.

He was a tormented, storm of a man, moody, over-sensitive, unstable, terrified of criticism and rejection, and yet; exceedingly rebellious. He tried desperately to control his strong sexual and drinking appetites, but was terribly unhappy with himself for his failure to do so. He was a man who couldn't be trusted, a con-artist, a user, whose friends were likely criminals. This man was out for himself and would do whatever he had to, to get what he wanted. This guy was dangerous.

Like Rosa, Marks was also confused. His confusion was caused in part by his involvement with many varied projects and activities. Though he started many things, he was weak willed and couldn't follow through with commitments. He was a quitter. He would get what he wanted in life by manipulation, by playing upon the weaknesses or vices of others.

When this man didn't get his way, he would use diplomacy, try to smooth talk his way. When that didn't work, his temper would explode. There would be violence. This was a man a woman would be smart to fear. He could have physically abused Rosa.

Together, Marks and Rosa had an interesting relationship. Marks fulfilled the authority figure Rosa needed in her life. He was domineering and had no problem telling Rosa what to do, which satisfied her.

Yet ironically, Marks was far more unstable and unpredictable than Rosa, who was more even tempered. Marks was everything Rosa should have naturally wanted to avoid. She couldn't trust people and he was a man who couldn't be trusted. The fact that she chose to be with such a man, fit perfectly. A woman who has learned that all people betray, naturally chooses the most untrustworthy man to reinforce her misconception.

Marks and Rosa had several things in common. Both were strategists who would have stimulated themselves by trying to outwit each other. Both liked an argument and were good in arguments. Both were loners and coveted their privacy. Both were self-conscious and feared rejection, and because of this, shunned society, kept to themselves, and avoided responsibilities. Though they were intelligent and had enough talent to do something meaningful with their lives, they would have rather not tried, than try and fail.

Both had artistic talent. Marks had literary capabilities and Rosa could have drawn, acted or played a muscial instrument. Both were interested in culture and would have enjoyed a good book, a play or music.

Unfortunately, both lacked direction, a sense of purpose and for this reason would have to exploit or depend upon others for whatever they wanted in life.

BOOK III

Chapter 13

In my life as a struggling songwriter I continued calling Hollywood, making appointments and dragging my guitar into the fancy offices on Sunset Boulevard where I sang for the men with gold records in their eyes. My confidence in my material had grown in proportion to the work I had put into my songwriting. When I was turned down now, I didn't walk away crushed. I believed in my music and I believed in my ability to write better music with time and work.

News had spread quickly among Hollywood publishers that a new writer was in town. Word had it that I was a good songwriter. Publishers welcomed me more warmly now.

Everyone in Hollywood has stories of great deals that fell through. I have several. Perhaps the one that hurt most was the deal I almost signed with a major publisher as a staff writer. I remember shaking the representative's hand and us agreeing that I would get $125 a week for writing songs. I was going to be the next Paul Simon he told me. His lawyer would draw up the papers. We would sign them Tuesday.

I waited for his call Tuesday, then I waited Wednesday. Thursday I called him. Things had changed, he told me. The deal had fallen through. But we shook hands, I said. Yea, but things had changed, he said. He was sorry.

I had already told everyone that I'd been hired as a staff writer and now I looked like a fool.

There were other disappointments but I will not bore you. I continued making appointments and driving to Hollywood. Afterwards, emotionally drained, I drove back to Pasadena, often praying each mile of the way that the car would not run out of gas. I had spent my last dollar on a hamburger.

Then coming home, checking the mailbox — a telephone bill and more returned tapes from publishers. Climbing the stairs, living on refried beans, corn tortillas and medium-hot salsa. My back aching, lying down, wondering how would I pay the phone bill — and, Lord, the rent was due two days ago. The awful night and the night worries. Did I really have talent as a songwriter, or was I fooling myself? Feeling uncertain, afraid, sometimes walking Colorado Boulevard for hours, that long street the Rose Parade meanders down each year across America's television sets. But there was no parade in the night. Just the lighted shop windows, the cars and other lonely men and women walking the night. I walked home, still feeling uncertain, reaching for the phone at one A.M., dialing the number, my friend waking on the other end, me needing assurance, sometimes breaking down, my friend tried to assure me.

I continued working at the pizza parlour serving beer and pouring root beers for high school girls with braces and two big, red pimples in the middle of their foreheads, and each girl with the eternal question: How much is a large root beer? — and the prices right in front of them.

One night, it all finally caved in, the feeling of failure knawing my pride like a rat at a hunk of cheese, I took the straw hat off, undid my apron and walked out the front door. That was it.

Afterwards, I wrote lead sheets for a major publisher whenever they had work. Suddenly, there was no more work and no more money and I was fed up with it all.

I moved back to Riverside and landed a five night a week gig. I had promised myself never to sing in bars again and there I was. But it was better than pouring beer for minimum wage.

Two weeks later I met a pretty, petite blonde. Her name was Edie. Four months later we were married. We bought a house and I was finally settled down.

My experiences in Hollywood had not destroyed my confidence. I was determined to succeed and I had a plan: build a recording studio, record an album, market the album at clubs, concerts and by independent record distributors. I began building the recording studio.

My wife Edie encouraged my musical endeavors and urged me to continue the Rosa May research which she was fascinated with. In fact, we spent several days of our honeymoon in Bodie where I led Edie to Rosa May's outcast grave and showed her the open field where Rosa's house had stood. We pitched our tent in the campground just north of the field. The September nights high in the Bodie Hills were already freezing and we were cold in our sleeping bags during the night but my wife did not complain. We spent the remainder of our honeymoon research-ing in Bridgeport, Carson City, Virginia City, Sacramento and San Francisco.

Over the next two years there were many research trips and my wife helped on all of them. We spent our entire summer vacations in the Eastern Sierras learning the history of the area, camping in Bodie for several days at a time. The Bodie nights were always cold and we shivered in our sleeping bags, clinging to one another for warmth as the fresh mountain air came in through the tent window.

We grew to love the old ghost town and the wild land in which it had sprung up. While standing on a mountain top, seeing for miles in every direction, the sky a smog-less royal blue, it was easy to understand why men and women came West and stayed. We knew they must have loved the sweet smelling sagebrush as we did, especially after the summer storms when thunderheads came fast on the wind and the rain fell full and hard, and afterwards the air smelling of the damp sage and wet earth. My wife and I loved that as we had loved the mountain flowers and learning their names: the red Indian Paintbrush, blue lupin, the fried-egg flowers, wild buckwheat and the yellow blooming rabbit brush.

We spend many hours in the courthouses and museums of Bridgeport, Carson City and Virginia City, checking and rechecking land records, police records, court records, births and deaths, coroner inquests, city directories —all in hopes of finding threads of Rosa May's life. It was hard work but it was satisfying work. We were diligent investigators and chased down every clue, hoping to find a fact in the end. Most of the chasing was fruitless, but there were always those times when we gleaned a new fact and another piece of Rosa May's puzzle was set in place.

Carson City and Virginia City, were especially important to us, for we knew these were places where Rosa had spent much time. When winter came, and we could not spend our money on research trips, and I had to write down what we had learned in the summer, we treasured our memories of the time spent in Carson and Virginia City. We remembered walking down Carson's Ormsby Street and the huge cottonwoods that shaded us from the sun as we searched and found the houses where Rosa May had long ago lived and worked. We remembered how tired we became after hours in the Carson Courthouse — when we had to break, driving down to the Carson River, and the water that came as far as our knees, and Harvey, our Springer Spaniel, swimming in the river with three boys, playing with them though they were strangers, and afterwards the boys building a fire beside the river to warm themselves.

In Virginia City we remembered walking down the creaking boardwalks, visiting the old saloons, especially the Delta Saloon, where a century earlier, Ernest Marks, Rosa's young lover, had spent much time. Later, walking down D Street, the old red light, to the cottonwood tree across from the Virginia and Truckee freight depot, where Cad Thompson's "Brick house" brothel once stood. There was a full moon that night and the bright silver light lit up D Street and the backs of saloons where stairs led down to the red light. We found ourselves imagining what life had really been like a hundred years earlier, here on D Street.

Later, we camped in the hills north of Virginia City where a hungry herd of cattle awakened and scared us in the night as they snorted and pulled at tufts of grass. We laughed afterwards but we were terrified at the time.

The search for Rosa May was exciting and interesting for my wife and I and we loved the old world it enfolded. My wife was very helpful, often coming up with new ideas and finding documents where I had previously and thoroughly searched.

There were two important questions about Rosa's life which we found difficult to answer: 1) when did she come to Bodie, and; 2) when did she die? Earlier in the research, I had felt that a deed could help pin-point the years Rosa had lived in Bodie. I had gone through Mono County records several times on my own in search of Rosa May owning property in Bodie. I had found nothing each time. Yet; intuitively, I believed that Rosa May had owned property. The deed that could prove so, was lost somewhere in the Bridgeport Courthouse. I was determined to find the deed.

In the meantime, I had found two important lists of early Bodie property owners. The first, was a list drawn up in 1880 when Bodie petitioned to incorporate. The second, was a list of property owners mentioned in the 1884 Bodie Fire Tax list. What is important about these lists is that they name the early Bodie red light operators.

My wife and I made a list of the early red light operators. We believed, that by tracing each name, we could discover who the early operators sold out to. Hopefully, Rosa May would eventually turn up. It was a long shot but it was worth a try.

Edie and I began patiently tracing each property owner in the Bridgeport Courthouse, going down the long lists of names in the huge Grantor-Grantee Indexes. We were tracing the name Rodriguez when my wife came across a scribbled name which appeared to be Rosa May.

It turns out that, a clerk had improperly filed Rosa's deed under her first name instead of her last.

In Book O, page 41, we found the deed. Dated June 14, 1902, it states that Rosa May purchased Lot 42 of Block 26 — directly in the red light — for $175 from a Hugh McCaghren. Here was documented proof that Rosa had owned land in Bodie, and proof that she was still alive in 1902.

But the deed provided us with one more gem: it states that Rosa May had occupied this house as a residence "upwards of ten years." This meant that she had more than likely permanently arrived in Bodie about 1892 at the age of thirty-eight.

Several things occurred about 1892 that may have stimulated Rosa's move from Carson and Virginia City to Bodie.

On May 27, 1892, Cad Thompson, the Virginia City madam that Rosa had long worked for, sold the "Brick house" to Jacob Tucker for $20. She had bought the same property in 1871 for $3,200. This gives you an idea how greatly Virginia City had declined.

In 1892, Cad Thompson was sixty-five. We know from Cad Thompson's letter to Rosa, dated March 27, 1880, that Thompson suffered from rheumatism. Virginia City's cold winters were hard on rheumatoid sufferers. It is believed that after running brothels thirty or more years in Virginia City, Cad Thompson was forced by financial difficulty and illness to sellout and retreat to San Francisco where she died some time later. Many vital records were destroyed in San Francisco's Great Fire and I was unable to locate Thompson's death certificate.

On February 2, 1893, Mary Ann Phillips, the Carson City madam who had often employed Rosa May, died at the age of seventy-one. Phillips was buried in Carson's Lone Mountain Cemetery beside Carson respectable folk. My wife and I located her grave and were taken back by the stone's heading. It read: Mother.

Phillips, a native of Nova Scotia, while running a brothel in Carson City, also owned a residence in Virginia City at 31 North B Street where it is believed she raised her children. The house at 31 North B Street still stands though her brothel in Carson at the corner of 4th and Ormsby has long been destroyed.

The demise of these two madams were not the only factors instrumental in Rosa's move to Bodie. Perhaps more importantly was the fact that the Comstock lode was no longer profitable for a prostitute, nor for anyone for that matter.

By 1893, Virginia City was gasping for its last breath. Mining companies reworked the old mines in efforts to rejuvenate the camp, reaping minor profits and bankruptcy. In the 1890's, John Mackay, one of the famous Silver Kings, who had made millions in Virginia City during the 1870's, finally sold all mining interests in the old camp.

The famous Territorial Enterprise, which had operated since 1860, sadly suspended publication. Dan DeQuille, noted Enterprise editor and writer, former roommate of Mark Twain, was forced to leave Virginia City, a place he had lived and worked in for over thirty years.

The decline of the Comstock mines in 1880 threw Nevada into a depression which lasted until shortly after the turn of the century. At that time, the southern camps of Tonopah and Goldfield boomed, breathing life and dollars into the Nevada economy.

Bodie in the 1890's was certainly in no better economic shape than the Comstock. Bodie's days as a boom camp were twenty years past. The camp would have perished had the cyanide process not been discovered and introduced into the Bodie mining facilities. This new process of gold extraction kept the camp alive and able to support a population of a thousand to fifteen hundred. That number would dwindle to eight hundred by 1900, and would dwindle further year by year until World War I, when mining ceased in Bodie for a time.

It would appear from the deed of 1902, that Rosa May permanently arrived in Bodie around 1893, and until that time, more than likely had continued working the brothels of Virginia and Carson City, and possibly Reno, which was only thirty miles from Carson. Her drifting to Bodie may not have been purely dictated by economics. At thirty-eight, after years of a precarious existence, jumping from one brothel to the next, perhaps Rosa longed for stability and permanence. The fact that Ernest Marks, Rosa's lover of her earlier years, was in Bodie; certainly had some effect on her decision to go to that camp.

New Years, 1880, is the last correspondence we have between Marks and Rosa May. It is not known what happened between them. It seems that they were separated a number of years. Ernest Marks was living in Bodie as early as March, 1884.

In March, 1884, several pages of the Lundy newspaper were given to a shooting involving Ernest Marks, Charlie Jardine, and Lundy Sheriff, Kirk Steves. Lundy was a mining camp some twenty-five miles southeast of Bodie.

From the article, it seems that Marks and Jardine were friends, though Jardine was known as a Bodie bad character. Apparently, there were bad feelings between Jardine and Kirk Steves. Steves egged Jardine into a fight. Several shots were fired by the three men, Marks being on Jardine's side. Jardine was shot in the leg. Marks and Steves escaped injury.

Ernest Marks was later arraigned in Bridgeport for the Lundy shooting. He was released and the matter was later dismissed.

Jardine was later shot and killed in Bodie. Kirk Steves suffered the same fate in Aurora in 1911, having threatened a saloon keeper. The writer of the Bridgeport Chronicle-Union article, claimed Steves was quarrelsome when drinking and was involved in several shooting scrapes. "Steves," the writer said, "when in liquor was continually threatening to kill someone and it is a surprise that he was not killed years ago."

The Lundy article went on to explain, that Ernest Marks worked for Morris Marks and Company, a wholesale liquor dealer in Bodie. Morris was Ernest's older brother and had left Gold Hill in 1879 when Bodie boomed and set up a permanent business there that year.

Morris Marks left Bodie in the late 1880's, at which time Ernest took over his saloon which he operated until 1919 when prohibition forced Ernest out of business.

In Bodie, Rosa lived in what was called the "lower end", or the Chinatown area. She rented the small white house on Bonanza Street which she later purchased. In 1900 there were about fifty Chinese still living in Chinatown. In 1893, there were certainly more.

Fifty feet from Rosa's front door, there was a corral, a stable and a small jail. Beyond this was Main Street at the foot of Bodie Bluff where the mines were located.

In coming to Bodie, Rosa had not placed herself in totally unfamiliar surroundings. Many of Bodie's citizens were men who had left the Comstock area when Virginia's mines played out. Some of these men became Bodie's principal businessmen. Antonio Maestretti, who ran a bakery in Virginia, became a saloon keeper in Bodie. Pete Tobin, who tended bar in Virginia, also opened his own saloon in Bodie. Harvey Boone, another ex-Virginian, operated a general store in Bodie. Jim Cain, who had worked in the Carson woodyards, became a banker and chief businessman. Hank Blanchard had operated a freight company between Carson and Bodie, later took over the Sunshine tollhouse between Bodie and Aurora. Many of Bodie's miners were also men who had worked Virginia's mines.

Mining camp people lived on the excitement and fast money of the boom camp. Due to the instability of the mining camp economy, men and women were forced to move on to the next camp when signs of decline appeared.

It is impossible to know exactly how many prostitutes were in Bodie in the 1890's. Had the entire 1890 Census not been destroyed by fire, we could have known the number. More than likely, there were no more than a handful.

It is apparent that Rosa's good friend, Emma Goldsmith, also ended up in Bodie in the 1890's. Goldsmith had operated a brothel in Carson City. She was arrested on several occasions, once for the use of opium. Her end was sad, as was the case of most prostitutes. August 18, 1900, Goldsmith was charged with the crime of insanity. She was released and eventually drank herself to death by October 13. A few brief lines in the Bridgeport Chronicle-Union marked her end:

Dead — Emma Goldsmith — one of Bodie's lowest levels, died about 3 o'clock this morning.

Emma Goldsmith had been a friend of Rosa's for over twenty years. Emma's sad death must have certainly given Rosa a foreshadowing of her own end.

By the dawn of the twentieth century, there were 141 red light districts in the country. By 1925, only one: Reno, Nevada. The red light districts of Minneapolis, Portland and Los Angeles would close by 1913, Denver by 1915. San Francisco's Barbary Coast, the Uptown Tenderloin, and New Orlean's Storyville would be closed in 1917.

The Golden Era of the American Brothel was coming to an end brought on by anti-prostitution groups, purity reform, the woman's suffrage movement, and the temperance movement. Women, the nation over, were taking an active part in ridding the family of those things which had often harmed it: alcohol, gambling, and prostitution.

The efforts of such movements were felt even in Bodie. In June, 1906, saloon keepers complained that Bodie was becoming a temperance town. July 13, 1907, Mono County Board of Supervisors passed an ordinance requiring saloon keepers to apply for liquor licenses quarterly, charging a one dollar license fee. The ordinance, aimed specifically at Bodie prostitutes, prohibited women in saloons and authorized the revoking of liquor licenses for law breakers. The ordinance was enforced January 13, 1912, when Antonio Maestretti and Ed Murphy lost their licenses for allowing women to frequent their saloons.

March 20, 1909, the Nevada legislature passed an anti-gambling amendment. In 1911 Mono County followed with Ordinance 113 which prohibited gambling in saloons. The ordinance forced gamblers to frequent the red light, where gambling was oddly allowed to continue. The Bridgeport Chronicle Union of August 19, 1911, attacked the gambling ordinance with fire:

Today there are as many men at work in the town of Bodie as there was a year ago. They receive the same wages as they did at that time and yet the town is dull. There has been no church revival, no man has been sent to the penitentiary for embezzlement or spending money that belonged to his creditors, yet the boys get rid of their money — and with people who pay neither taxes or license.

One year ago there were two or three houses of prostitution and about the same number of inmates. Now there are four times as many and the red lights burn till dawn. The men who were in the habit of playing a game or two of cards in a saloon now spend their money in less desirable places.

...Bodie is a mining camp. It has no theaters, parks, library or other place where a single man can spend his idle hours. For the young man the open saloon is better than the red light district and Chinatown.

Gambling behind closed doors is patronized more fully by young men than it is that in a public place, and the crooked gambler is always present in such a place. If Ordinance No. 113 has improved the moral status of Bodie (the place in Mono County at which it was aimed) the betterment is not visible ... it is a breeder of crime, compelling hypocrisy and making a bad matter worse...

However; the gambling ordinance was not revoked and Bodie prostitutes continued reaping its benefits.

In 1880, one third of California's population were women, a large number of these were prostitutes who had helped to settle California during the gold rush. By 1900, however; there were many respectable women, more families. Prostitution posed a threat to these.

On April 7, 1913, after hard pressure from anti-prostitition groups, the California legislature passed the Red Light Abatement Act. The act states that, "Every building or place used for immoral purposes is a nuisance which shall be enjoined, abated and prevented as hereinafter provided, whether the same be public or private nuisance." The act also levied fines and/or imprisonment for the owners of such property; the removal and sale of all furnishings (including musical instruments) and the closing of the building to any occupancy for one year.

The Red Light Abatement Act went on the November 1914 ballot as a referendum. The people of California voted the referendum into law which became effective December 19, 1914. The law, however, was resisted and was considered unconstitutional by many. But in 1917, the California Supreme Court decided that the Red Light Abatement Act was constitutional. So began the crack-down on all California red light districts.

Ironically, the strong wave of anti-prostitition sentiment came as Rosa May neared the end of her life in Bodie, California.

We found it very difficult to determine exactly when Rosa May died. Mono County death records go back as far as the 1860's. Mysteriously they were without record of Rosa's death. Rosa had died after 1902 and county clerks were more diligent at that time than predecessors. There should have been a death certificate.

Evidently, the attending physician— if there had been one, did not file a death certificate. Rosa's friends had not nor the undertaker.

Furthermore; Mono County health records were without history of epidemics which made it impossible to pinpoint the Bodie pneumonia epidemic which supposedly claimed Rosa's life.

I later learned that after 1900, vital statistics for every county in California were sent to Sacramento and recorded by the Bureau of Vital Statistics. I contacted the Bureau and had them search their records between 1900-18 for a death of Rosa May. They found nothing.

Finally, I searched through every newspaper published in the Bodie area between 1900-18 in hopes of finding a mention of Rosa's death. These newspapers included: the **Bridgeport Chronicle-Union;** Hawthorne's, **Walker Lake Bulletin;** the **Aurora Borealis;** Mina, Nevada's, **Western Nevada Miner** and the few remaining issues of the **Bodie Miner.**

While searching the November 17, 1906 issue of the **Bridgeport Chronicle-Union,** I thought I had finally found what I was looking for. Under "Bodie Items" there were these brief lines:

A woman resident of Chinatown died Sunday evening at 8 o'clock coroner's inquest was held Monday by Judge Moyle and the jury failed to agree as to the cause of her death. On Tuesday a postmortem examination revealed the fact that alcoholism was the cause of her death. The body was buried in Potter's field Tuesday by friends.

The item contained all the important facts: Chinatown woman, obviously a prostitute, dies of alcoholism, is burried by friends in Potter's field — the outcast cemetery.

In the Bridgeport Courthouse I searched for the coroner's inquest, to discover whether or not the woman was in fact Rosa May. I did not find the inquest.

Later, I learned a Molly Piantoni appeared on the 1905-06 delinquent tax list. Piantoni had owned lots 39 and 40 of Block 26 in the red light. It would seem from this information, that Molly Piantoni was the prostitute who had died of alcoholism. Several things pointed to this:

In his, **Mining Camp Days**, Emil Billeb mentions that Rosa May, along with Big Bonanza, Big Nell and Bull Con Josey, were the Bodie prostitutes when Billeb arrived in 1908 to take over management of the Bodie and Benton railroad. Emil Billeb is dead, but those who knew him, claim that he had a marvelous memory. Billeb's information coincides with that of Sadie Cain and Anna McKenzie who remember seeing Rosa as late as 1910.

I believe Rosa May died between November, 1911 and November, 1912. Her property appeared on the 1912-13 Mono County delinquent tax list. Her property tax had become delinquent November, 1912. The property went up for tax sale on June, 1913 and was assessed at a value of $210, $35 more than the 1902 purchase price. In 1918, Rosa's property was sold to the State of California. Her house and other red light and Chinatown buildings were torn down by 1919.

The Bodie Miner more than likely mentioned Rosa's death. Unfortunately I was unable to find the particular issue. Some twelve years earlier Lyin' Jim Townsend, editor of the paper, had been a friend of Rosa's but had left Bodie around 1899.

The Bridgeport Chronicle-Union was an extremely conservative paper. Yet; in the past, it had carried the deaths of prostitutes — even squaws, then considered lower than prostitutes. But the Chronicle-Union did not mention Rosa May's death. One wonders why.

A handful of Bodie women had managed to force men to bury Rosa outside the fence, but the Chronicle-Union — always hard up for news — gave Rosa May the final humiliating blow by not mentioning her death.

The last interesting pieces of information come from two old timers, Guy McInnis and Herb DeChambeau, who lived in Bodie before and after the turn of the century.

Throughout my research, I was often told that Guy McInnis was the oldest survivor of Bodie's earlier days. I had written him several times, each time my letter was returned with a polite note that said Mr. McInnis was quite elderly, nearly blind, and of no help to me besides. But I didn't believe that and managed to get Guy's phone number from a daughter-in-law.

Guy now lived in Las Vegas and I called him there. I introduced myself and asked Guy about turn of the century Bodie and Rosa May. I soon learned that Guy knew more than he thought he knew. I persuaded him to allow me to interview him. Several days later my wife and I drove two hundred and fifty miles to Las Vegas.

We stayed the night in Vegas before interviewing Guy the next morning. During the night I became very sick for no apparent reason. The next morning we had an awful time finding Guy's house. After an hour's search, we found it, a green stucco house in a middle-class neighborhood whose streets were scrambled like a rat maze.

Guy McInnis, born in 1882, was ninety-five. He was pale and silver haired. He had a sharp mind and a good memory but unfortunately his eyes were very bad and he was unable to identify pictures of Bodie. As I spoke with 'him he tapped his fingers nervously on his rocking chair and breathed heavily. He was polite and tried hard to remember things I asked about. Guy wanted to know what I was going to do with the information so I told him.

As a young man, Guy worked as a clerk in Cecil Burkham's general store. Burkham's carried everything, groceries, candy, hardware, dry goods, Christmas things and fruits in season.

The telephone was brought to Bodie around 1900. The red light women would phone Burkham, place their orders and Guy would deliver them because the red light women seldom came uptown. He had heard that the prostitutes sometimes frequented the saloons at night, but Guy could not recall them doing so.

It was on his deliveries to the red light district that Guy saw Rosa May a few times. He says that Rosa was, "a very quiet woman... not very handsome, stout as far as I remember, short and stout. Must have been in her forties. Don't remember what color hair she had. It was common knowledge in Bodie that Marks lived down there with her." When I asked Guy how the townspeople felt about that, Guy said, "They didn't pay any attention to it as far as I know."

"Marks", he said, "ouside of running his saloon didn't mix with society. He was bummed up with rheumatism. I know he walked with a cane. Now Neuman Tobias, his bartender, was something like Marks himself. Fifty years of age or more, quiet sort of man. He was a Jew too."

As far as Guy knew, Rosa had continued in prostitution as long as Marks lived with her. He insisted that Rosa was never a madam.

There were about four houses of prostitution in Bodie at the time. Emma Goldsmith's place was just north of Jim Cain's bank, near the corner of King and Main Street, back a ways and facing main.

Guy could not remember Rosa's death nor the pneumonia

epidemic which was supposed to have taken her life. He did say there was a year when the "grip" was real bad.

"That must have been a curious crowd up there that made them dig her grave outside," Guy said. "It's just like the Lord said, 'Let ye without sin cast the first stone.' I can't see why they had to bury her there. She didn't contaminate the ground a' tall."

That was all Guy could remember. He wished he could have remembered more and apologized for not being able to. I told him he had helped us an awful lot. He carefully walked us out to our car, this kind old man who was nearly blind. He seemed so lonely as we left him and he stood and watched our car as we drove away. He looked to me like a willow that had bent so much in so many years that he was simply tired of bending.

Guy McInnis died two weeks later.

Herb DeChambeau was born in the Bodie area in 1888. He was 88 when my wife and I interviewed him in San Diego. He had lived a long, full life, with many varied adventures which he spoke excitedly about. He had driven hay teams and stages, broke horses and hiked up mountains carrying ninety pounds of mail. He had been a cowboy, a miner, a millman in Bodie's Standard Mill. He had joined up as a bugler in the Spanish American War, and sought excitement as a soldier, volunteering for the Canadian Army in 1916. He had had a good life and talked of it full of zest and humor in a raspy voice as he stretched himself on the bed where he spent most of his time. The three of us sipped whisky and soda which Herb had eagerly and generously poured out. Laid up like he was now that he was older, the whisky seemed to help Herb remember the days when he lived in Bodie shortly before the camp's demise.

Herb told us of Bodie's big saloons, how the sawdust covered the floor and a beer cost ten cents a mug, five for a Pony schooner; how all the saloon keepers laid out meat, cheese and bread on the counter for the popular free lunches. He told us about Marks' saloon, how Marks, like Seiler another saloon keeper, was very stand-offish. Marks was about 57, medium build, mustached and grey haired.

Herb lived in Bodie in 1898 and 99, and 1908 up through the fall of 1911. He and the "boys" had often frequented the Bodie red light, or "Angel's roost" as he called it.

It was there in the Bodie red light between 1908 and 1911, that Herb met Rosa May, who was about fifty, and too old for prostitution, he claims. She had three or four girls working for her. A beer went for two bits — a quarter — and two dollars paid for a good time with one of Rosie's girls in the backroom.

Marks lived "down there" with Rosa and everyone knew about it. Marks, however; never talked about Rosa.

It is interesting that Herb Dechambeau remembered Rosa as a madam.

The Bridgeport Cronicle-Union carried these lines December, 1909:

The tent house in which Rosie and her girls are living caught on fire last Sunday. One end of the tent was burned out and most of their clothing burnt. It is not known how the fire started.

This fire took place in Masonic, a gold camp fifteen miles from Bodie which had a population at this time of about five hundred lonely, sex starved men. Very likely, the Rosie mentioned was Rosa May who apparently, had employed several girls.

Several things would account for this: One, Rosa was no longer the good looking woman of earlier years. Secondly, the recent excitement of Masonic and Lucky Boy had increased Mono County population by eight hundred, many of these, single men employed by the new mines. There was, therefore; more money to be made from prostitution. Third, the recent banning of saloon gambling had increased the popularity of the red light districts, also adding to the prostitution profit. Certainly, these factors must have encouraged Rosa May to bring in younger prostitutes from the outside.

From this, it seems that Rosa May might have been a madam for a short period toward the end of her life.

Chapter 14

*Greater love hath no man than this, that a
man lay down his life for his friends.*
John 15:13

It was early morning and very cold. A thin sheet of frost lay on our tent, and when we exhaled, a stream of white vapor blew from our lips. The sun's yellow rays lit up parts of the valley but its warmth had not reached us yet, as the campground lay in the cold, dark shadow of Bodie Bluff. I was hoping the sun would rise quickly over the mountain, but I knew it would, take some time. While my wife slept buried in her sleeping bag, I quietly slipped from the tent. I was wanting fire and a good cup of hot chocolate.

I pumped the Coleman stove vigourously, then turned the black knob that allowed the gas fumes into the burner. The fumes, white from the cold, sputtered out the black holes. I struck a match and the fumes puffed into a greenish-blue flame. Fire at last. I warmed my cold hands over the flames.

Nearby, there is a spring that runs year round. I filled a copper-bottomed saucepan with cold spring water, heated it on the Coleman and poured the steaming water into two cups partially filled with instant hot chocolate. I woke my wife and brought the hot chocolate to her and we talked about how cold it was.

It was September again high in the Bodie Hills. We were the only campers foolish or poor enough to brave the cold, Bodie night in a nylon tent.

When we finished the hot chocolate, we put our wool-knit caps on and bundled ourselves in sweaters and jackets. I grabbed the hand-axe and photos. My wife brought the camera, and Harvey, our Springer Spaniel, ran ahead of us as we walked around the ghost town, south to the cemetery. This early in the morning, no one would disturb us.

Late in the afternoon of the previous day, my wife and I had been working in the cemetery, searching for Rosa's actual grave which had been lost over the years. The sky grew somber with brooding, black clouds and it began to rain. I didn't want the photos to get wet so we took shelter in the nearby morgue.

I was disturbed that afternoon by our repeated bad luck which seemed to always overtake us in Bodie. Our car, which ran fine over mountains and desert, suddenly developed mechanical problems in Bodie on several occasions, faulty fuel pumps, flat tires, sudden shortages of gas and oil, and finally, a thrown rod. Always in Bodie, nowhere else.

I felt that something wanted to frustrate or hamper our progress. This feeling became more eerie when I remembered how on several occasions, I had felt a dark, oppressive force while standing beside Rosa's grave. Our repeated bad luck in Bodie and this dark feeling caused me to secretly believe that this **something** did not want Rosa's story to be made known. And now the rain, when we were so close to locating Rosa's grave.

But on this morning, the sky was clear and there were no signs of rain. I prayed that we would have good luck with our search.

We climbed the sagebrush slopes to the outcast cemetery where I left my wife while Harvey and I continued up the hill, through the regular cemetery, to the place Burton Frasher shot his 1927 photos. These were the only early photos of Bodie cemetery showing Rosa's picket fence just outside the cemetery. Positioning myself at the point where Frasher had taken his photos, I would try again to pinpoint Rosa's grave by comparing landmarks in the cemetery with landmarks in the town beyond.

I was now some two hundred yards from my wife. "Walk that

way," I yelled, and pointed which direction. "Keep going." I looked at the photos again. "Now come forward. More. More. That's right." I studied the photos once again. "Now a little to your left. Alright. Stay there, I think that's it." I ran down through the cemetery, dodging graves and sagebrush, to my wife. Sure enough, where she stood, there was a small mound of dirt covered by sagebrush, the trunk of which, was as thick as my forearm. I grabbed the hand-axe and chopped the brush away. The small mound was obviously the grave of a tiny woman. My wife and I smiled. I raised my arms up victoriously. "This is it. This is her grave," and we were so happy to have found it.

Louis Serventi's concrete marker stood some one hundred and fifty feet northwest of Rosa's actual grave. Though Serventi had misplaced his marker, it was his gravestone that had stimulated my curiousity. I was grafetul. Had he not made the marker, I likely would have never become interested in Rosa's legend.

It had all begun here in the outcast cemetery, and it seemed fitting that it should end here. My wife and I gathered large stones and piled them on the tiny mound so Rosa's grave would not be lost again.

As I stood there by Rosa's grave, I felt great satisfaction for having begun the search and for having stuck with it for as long as it had taken. We had gone through every courthouse record, police record, newspaper, census; read every book and article; and interviewed many people seekng information of the legend of Rosa May. Now, the work was all done. There was nothing more to check. We felt relieved.

It was here in the mining camp of Bodie, in this green mountain valley below barren bluffs, that Rosa Elizabeth White — who later called herself, Rosa May; had died in the winter months of 1911-1912 at the age of fifty-seven, having spent forty-one years of her life as a prostitute. They had dragged her coffin by sled up the snowy slopes and buried her here in the outcast cemetery, some hundred feet outside the fence. A picket fence was placed around her grave which was eventually destroyed by weather or stolen. No stone was placed on her grave. No newspaper had mourned her passing. No document had marked her end. It seemed as if the world made believe that Rosa May had never lived. But she had, and there were reasons for her living as she had.

Born in 1855, a daughter of Irish immigrants, Rosa May was a wonderfully warm, inquisitive child who had the misfortune of having been born into a terribly suppressive, unstable home. Misunderstanding and the ill treatment by her parents, bred in Rosa feelings of worthlessness and guilt which dominated and motivated her life. Due to this ill treatment, she would never lead a happy, normal life.

In 1871, at the age of sixteen, Rosa ran away from her home in Pennsylvania. She drifted to New York City where she fell in with a hard crowd of young men and women as badly damaged as herself. Soon, she was prostituting to survive, a choice made freely, aware of what she was doing. In prostitution, she found a place to belong among other homeless, souls like herself. She drifted into a bizarre, lonely world of superficial relationships — a life without bottom, in which men and women used each other mercilessly.

In 1871, having heard of the good money to be made in mining camps, Rosa May, like thousands of eastern prostitutes, went west. She worked the mining camp brothels of Colorado and Idaho for two years. In 1873, she hit Virginia City, Nevada, just in time for the fantastic boom of 1874. She worked the Virginia City, Carson City and Reno circuit of whorehouses for the next twenty years and eventually drifted to Bodie in the early 1890's where she lived until her death in 1911-12. In the few years before her death, she may have earned her living as a madam. However; the majority of evidence implies that she was an ordinary prostitute to the end.

About 1877, she met Ernest Marks in Virginia City. Rosa and Marks fell in love and remained lovers while Rosa continued prostituting. In the early 1880's it appears they separated, Marks moving on to Bodie with his brother Morris. Their relationship resumed when Rosa came to Bodie about 1893.

From '93 until her death, Rosa and Marks had a steady relationship. Marks lived with her in the red light as Rosa continued in prosititution. Rosa May was loyal and tenacious which accounts for her sticking with Marks, though he was unstable, ill-tempered and violent.

After Rosa's death, in spite of the years they had spent together, Marks never laid a fitting monument upon Rosa's grave. He took up with other Bodie prostitutes who eventually robbed and left him. He spent the last years of his life crippled by arthiritis. He was often seen hobbling along the boardwalks, leaning on his ever present cane. In 1919, prohibition drove Marks out of the saloon business. He lived in his saloon alone, supported by relatives in the east, until his death in 1928. Though legend claims he was buried beside Rosa, his death certificate states that he was buried in the Odd Fellows cemetery, within the fence. His grave remains unmarked.

There was little evidence that Rosa May died while nursing miners during one of Bodie's pneumonia epidemics. Newpapers, always looking for interesting items, carried no stories of the supposed epidemic. County health records were poorly kept and could not substantiate the Bodie epidemic. Memories of old timers were void of such a recollection.

Despite this, old timers persistently remembered Rosa May as a "good hearted" woman who helped the poor whenever she could. A graphoanalysis of her handwriting substantiates this claim: Rosa May was a woman who could be easily tempted to sacfifice herself for others.

How then, had Rosa died? The epidemic Ella Cain spoke of may have actually been three or four men who came down with pneumonia. Perhaps Rosa May, known for her good heart, generous by nature, had gone to these men— most likely neighbors, had nursed them and perished in the process. There was nothing, really, to prove that she had. Then again, there was nothing to prove that she hadn't.

Rosa May was an ordinary mining camp prostitute and her life followed the general pattern of such women. A confused young girl, emotionally damaged, without ambition or hope for her life, she had gone into prositiution. There she found easy money and others like herself. With youth and beauty on her side, prostitution was profitable and more bearable. But with the passing years, the grueling life eventually robbed Rosa of her beauty. Profits dwindled, prostitution became a harder way of life. Many prostitutes during the declining years had killed themselves. Rosa May had not. She had gone into the life freely. Loyal and tenacious, she had stuck it out until the very end.

Chapter 15

We dig four holes, one at each corner of Rosa's grave. My wife and I and a young park ranger lift the fence posts into the four holes. With a shovel, I bury the posts with dirt and rock. The fence is a replica of the picket fence torn from her grave. I used old weathered lumber to give it an aged look.

Now that the fence is in place, I take hold of it with my hand and give it a shake. Strong enough. I hope it will survive the hard Bodie winters and the pack rat instincts of curious visitors.

It's a hot August day in Bodie. I wipe the sweat from my forehead with my open hand. I motion to my wife for the canteen. She hands it to me. I take a long swallow of the good, sweet spring water.

The sky is very blue. Huge cotton ball clouds, like great white birds, hang in the sky. Every time we've come to this country we've found it more difficult to return to the smoggy skies and rat race life in Southern California.

Looking down the slopes from Rosa's grave you can see it all. It's pretty much the same as the first time I came to Bodie. The weathered, tobacco colored buildings stand like a ruin in the green fields. Many visitors walk the fields and the dirt streets. Grownups and children on tip-toes, hands on windowsills, peak inside the old buildings. They are seeking the ancient people who lived here. They peek through windows as if hoping to look through time and see and feel and hear how it was when Bodie was the roaring mining camp that later became legend. But the ancient people they seek are dead and gone. The curious visitors find only those discarded things that couldn't find room in the cramped wagons and trucks when families pulled out of Bodie after the mines closed. Through the windows they see stained mattresses, broken chairs, dusty chest-of-drawers, a wood burning stove, faded newspapers and such. The imagination of these curious souls is stirred. They would love to see Bodie alive once again. But they will have to settle for this ghost town, with its dusty memories and fading stories.

Cars, trucks and campers jostle to and fro over the bone-white, dirt road below the cemetery. The kicked-up dust floats on the wind in a cloud. Some visitors are on their way out, back to the highway. Others are arriving, slowly rocking toward the large parking lot a quarter mile from the cemetery. In the parking lot, moms and dads, kids and grand-parents, pile out for their first glimpse of a real ghost town.

Casually dressed in jeans, shorts and T-shirts, visitors walk the worn paths of the Bodie cemetery. With cameras about their necks, they speak excitedly of the strange wooden planks used to mark the graves, now split and faded with the years. Here, wooden fences are toppled over, graves are overrun with sagebrush, sturdy stone markers have names and dates neatly carved. The visitors count the life spans on their fingers, seeking the earliest death or the oldest human being. Many are touched by the number of children buried in the Bodie Cemetery.

Here, are buried the many men who died in the mines during Bodie's fifty year life. Some men were blown up through a negligent use of dynamite. Some fell hundreds of feet down dark mine shafts. Some were victims of heat exhaustion, cave-ins, runaway ore cars. These men had gambled their lives in the mines and they had lost their bets.

In the far southwest corner of the cemetery, visitors find a strong black iron fence surrounding an unmarked grave. This is the grave of Lottie Johl, the prostitute who married Eli Johl, the butcher. Lottie died November 7, 1899, after taking a prescription that was accidentally filled with poison. She was forty-four and had come a long way from her home in Iowa to die in this rugged mining camp.

Eli fought hard to have Lottie buried inside the cemetery. The townspeople were opposed. But Lottie was no longer a prostitute Eli raged. Lottie was his wife and she would be buried inside the cemetery.

Eli won his fight. The townspeople grudgingly allowed Lottie burial inside the fence — but only in the remotest part of the cemetery, farthest from the entrance, here in the southwest corner.

And there beside Rosa's white marker a man and wife and their ten year old daughter act out a scene I've witnessed several times. The husband and wife hold hands as they stand before Rosa's marker. They study the child-like letters. They notice that there are no dates nor place of birth. The paint has been blasted from the stone by hard weather.

"This is the woman we learned about in the museum," the husband says.

"The red light woman," the wife asks.

"Uh-huh."

"What's a red light woman, Daddy?"

"Oh, ... that means she was ... a prostitute."

"What?"

"Never mind Kate. You'll learn about those things soon enough," her mother says.

"Dad, c'mon. What was she?"

"She was a woman who probably had a hard life."

"Oh." The girl ponders her father's words. She spots a cluster of wild daisies near Rosa's grave. The girl kneels and tenderly pulls them from the earth. She lays them at the foot of Rosa's marker. "There," she says, with obvious satisfaction.

The wife turns, and looks down at the ghost town and the barren hills beyond. "How could any woman live in a place like this?"

"I don't know."

The man and his wife turn from Rosa's grave and begin walking down the hill to the road that leads back to their car. The girl remains beside Rosa's grave, thinking about Rosa May and what she was. A strange loneliness she has never felt surrounds her.

"Katie, c'mon," her father calls. The girl runs down the hill dodging the clumps of sagebrush. Reaching her parents she takes hold of her father's hand. She leans close to him and whispers, "You'll tell me what she was later, won't you?" The father looks at his daughter and smiles. He remembers how curious he was. "Katie, like Mom says, you're too young to know about some things. I know you don't understand that. We're just thinking of you. When you're older, if you still want to know, I'll tell you." Katie's face crumples.

"Oh, alright," she moans. Her father smiles. He wraps his arms around his two favorite girls and pulls them close.

"I love you," he says.

About the Author

Since the publication of *Rosa May* in 1979, George Williams III has written ten books. A second book on prostitution, *The Redlight Ladies of Virginia City, Nevada*, 1984, includes more information about Rosa May and the prostitution underworld in Virginia City during the mining boom years, 1860-1900.

The Guide to Bodie and Eastern Sierra Historic Sites, 1982, tells the story of the rise and fall of Bodie and includes nearly 100 photographs of the famous gold mining town and other contemporary mining camps.

More information about Virginia City can be found in Williams' *Mark Twain: His Life In Virginia City, Nevada*, 1986, the second in a three part Mark Twain in the West Series. Other books in the series are *Mark Twain: Mining Days at Aurora and Mono Lake*, 1987, and *Mark Twain: The Making of the "Jumping Frog of Calaveras County*,*"* 1988. Mr. Williams is currently completing another in the series, *On The Road With Mark Twain In California and Nevada*, a travel guide to Twain's haunts in the West.

The Murders At Convict Lake, 1984, tells the story of an infamous 1871 Nevada State Penitentiary escape which resulted in numerous killings, a 200 mile posse chase and the hanging of two convicts.

A good chunk of Mr. Williams' knowledge of the music business is in *The Songwriter's Demo Manual and Success Guide*, 1984, which *Booklist* described as, "the most helpful guide of its kind...A valuable, well organized handbook and a cogent look at a tough show-business field."

Hot Springs of the Eastern Sierra, 1988, is Williams' humorous guide to 40 natural hot springs.

Williams' newest, best and funniest book, *In The Last of The Wild West*, 1991, is the true story of his efforts to expose political corruption in Storey County, Nevada where Williams published the notorious *Virginia City Voice* newspaper in Virginia City. Storey

County government is controlled by a notorious brothel operator whom Williams "took on." Williams' explosive satires nearly caused him to get his "damned head blown off," says Williams. "Well, the closest I ever got to being hanged or shoved down the nearest mine shaft, anyway."

In 1981 Williams was nominated for the Commonwealth Club of California Literary Award for *Rosa May*. In 1986 his book, *Mark Twain: His Life In Virginia City, Nevada*, was selected as a nominee for the Pulitizer Prize in Letters.

Today George Williams III is one of the America's best selling authors. He lives in northwestern Nevada where he hopes to stay unless he's "run out for writing the truth."

Acknowledgments

A great big thanks to the following old-timers who were cornered and interrogated.

In Bridgeport: Slick Bryant, Marceline Bryant (for cookies and milk), Stuart and Sadie Cain, Helen and Walter Evans, George Delury, W. Lee Symonds(fine artist.)

In Mono City: Frank Balfe

Bishop: Nellie Blye O'Brian, Richie Conway, Margherita Milovich and Louise, Anna McKenzie, Louis Serventi.

San Francisco: Charles Ah Yuen Kee.

Oakland: Bill Glenn.

San Diego: Herb Dechambeau.

Yerington: Mrs.Bell, Markham Trailkill.

Carson City: Noreen Humphries for helping me to locate properties, Burd Lindsey, for pointing out houses of prostitution.

Virginia City: Kate Tanahill, Father H.G. Champlin, St. Mary's in the Mountains, for checking Catholic hospital records.

Las Vegas: Guy McInnis, gone home now.

Special thanks to the following: Frank Wedertz (author, **Bodie: 1859-1900)** for sharing so much with me about Bodie and Bridgeport history. My deepest thanks for encouragement and editing advice.

Roberta Wedertz, for hospitality and great home cooked meals. We owe you.

Dan Bryant, Mono County Assessor, for aid in locating Bodie properties and for use of Bodie newspapers.

Staff of the Mono County Clerk's Office and Mono County Sheriff.

Graphonanalysts, Judy Craig and Verna Lea-Turner. You opened the door.

John Cahoon, Los Angeles Museum of Natural History.

Father Harold F. Vieages, Lovelock, Nevada, Archivist.

Appreciation to the following for information and research aid: Bob and Ardie Adkisson, Henry Raub, Warren Loose, J. McClaren Forbes, Dick Russell, Jack Geyer and Steve Medley, Clay Calhoun, Briscoe Honea, Chloe Clay, Carl Chafin, Anthony Knapp, Gary Howard.

My thanks to Holt, Rinehart and Winston for allowing me to reprint passages from, **A HOUSE IS NOT A HOME,** by Polly Adler.

A big thank you to Harry Lawton, Frank Wedertz and Kevin Lamb for reading the manuscript and giving honest editing suggestions. You really helped.

Thank you Lord Jesus for showing me the way.

Bibliography

The following is a list of records from which documented information was obtained.

United States Federal Census: Mono County, California 1880 and 1900; Storey County, Nevada 1860, 1870, 1880; Ormsby County, Nevada 1870 and 1880.

Federal Passport Records, Washington, D.C.

State Records: California Bureau of Vital Statistics, 1875 Nevada State Census.

City and County: Birth, death, voting and police records of Mono County, California; Storey and Ormsby County, Nevada.

Church Records: Methodist and Catholic.

Early California and Nevada newspapers provided by the Bancroft Library and the Nevada State Library:

> Aurora Borealis
> Bodie Evening Miner
> Bridgeport Chronicle-Union
> Carson Appeal
> Territorial Enterprise
> Virginia City Evening Chronicle
> Walker Lake Bulletin
> Western Nevada Miner

My thanks to the following libraries: city libraries of Riverside, Carson City, Pasadena, Pomona, and Bridgeport. State libraries, California and Nevada; Bancroft Library, Berkeley; the Genealogical Library of the Mormon Church, Los Angeles and the University of California, Riverside library. Also Washington University library, Carl Parcher Russell papers.

Museums: Bodie Museum, Dayton Museum; Eastern Calif. Museum, Los Angeles County Museum of Natural History, Mono County Museum, Nevada State Museum.

The following books were helpful:

Adler, Polly: **A HOUSE IS NOT A HOME.** New York: Holt, Rinehart and Winston Inc. 1953

Arnold, Emmett L.: **GOLD CAMP DRIFTER.** University of Nevada Press. 1973

Asbury, Herbert: **THE BARBARY COAST.** Garden Publishing Co., New York. 1933

Beebe, Lucius and Clegg, Charles: **LEGENDS OF THE COMSTOCK LODE.** Stanford University Press. 1950

Benjamin, Harry and Masters, R.E.L.: **PROSTITUTION AND MORALITY.** Julian Press Inc., New York. 1964

Billeb, Emil: **MINING CAMP DAYS,** Howell-North Books, Berkeley. 1968

Bunker, M.N.: **HANDWRITING ANALYSIS: THE SCIENCE OF DETERMINING PERSONALITY BY GRAPHO-ANALYSIS.** Nelson-Hall Co., Chicago. 1966

Cain, Ella: **THE STORY OF BODIE.** Fearon Publishers, San Francico. 1956

Cain, James M.: **PAST ALL DISHONOR.** Alfred A. Knopf. New York. 1946

Choisy, Maryse: **PSYCHOANALYSIS OF THE PROSTITUTE.** Philosophical Library, New York. 1961

Cousins, Sheila: **TO BEG I AM ASHAMED.** The Richards Press, London. 1953

Danberg, Grace: **CARSON VALLEY.** Carson Valley Historical Society, 1972

De Quille, Dan: **THE BIG BONANZA.** 1876 Hartford, Conn. 1947 Alfred A. Knopf, New York

Doten, Alfred: **THE JOURNALS OF ALFRED DOTEN,** 1849-1903. Edited by Walter Van Tilburg. University of Nevada Press, Reno

Drury, Wells: **AN EDITOR ON THE COMSTOCK LODE.** Pacific Books, Palo Alto. 1936

Elliot, Russell R.: **HISTORY OF NEVADA.** University of Nebraska Press. 1973.

Fisher, Vardis: **CITY OF ILLUSION.** Harper and Bros., New York. 1941.

Gentry, Curt: **THE MADAMS OF SAN FRANCISCO.** Doubleday and Co., New York. 1964.

Greenwald, Harold: **THE ELEGANT PROSTITUTE.** Walker and Company, New.York. 1970.

Hoffer, Eric: **THE TRUE BELIEVER.** Harper and Row, New York. 1951

Hulse, James W.: **THE NEVADA ADVENTURE.** University of Nevada Press, Reno. 1965

Kimball, Nell: **NELL KIMBALL: HER LIFE AS AN AMERICAN MADAM.** Edited by Stephen Longstreet. Macmillan Co., New York. 1970

Lewis, Flannery: **SUNS GO DOWN.** Macmillan Company, New York. 1937

Lewis, Oscar: **SILVER KINGS.** Alfred A. Knopf, New York. 1947

Loose, Warren: **BODIE BONANZA.** Exposition Press, Jericho, New York. 1971

Lord, Elliot: **COMSTOCK MINING AND MINERS.** 1883, reprint, Howell-North books, Berkeley. 1959

Martin, Cy: **WHISKEY AND WILD WOMEN.** Hart Publishing Co., Inc., New York. 1974

Miller, Max: **HOLLADAY STREET,** 1960

Milner, Christina and Richard: **BLACK PLAYERS.** Little, Brown and Company, Boston/Toronto. 1972

Murtagh, John M and Harris Sara: **CAST THE FIRST STONE.** McGraw-Hill Book Co., New York. 1957

Osborne, Lewis: **THE LIFE AND TIMES OF THE VIRGINIA CITY TERRITORIAL ENTERPRISE.** Edited by Oscar Lewis, Ashland, Oregon. 1972

Paher, Stanley W.: **NEVADA GHOST TOWNS AND MINING CAMPS.** Howell-North Books, Berkeley, California.

Pearson, Michael: **THE 5 VIRGINS.** Saturday Review Press, New York. 1972

Pivar, David J.: **SEXUAL MORALITY AND SOCIAL CONTROL,** 1868-1900. Greenwood Press Inc., Westport, Conn./London, England.

Rasmussen, Louis: **RAILWAY PASSENGER LISTS OF OVERLAND TRAINS TO SAN FRANCISCO AND THE WEST.**

Rose, Al: **STORYVILLE NEW ORLEANS.** University of Alabama Press. 1974

Russell, Carl Parcher: **"The Bodie that Was."** Touring Topics, November, 1929.

Sheehy, Gail: **HUSTLING.** Dell Publishing Company Inc.. 1971

Smith, Grant H.: **THE HISTORY OF THE COMSTOCK LODE,** 1850-1920. Nevada State Bureau of Mines and the Mackay School of Mines, 1943

Stern, Jess: **SISTERS OF THE NIGHT.** Julian Messner, Inc., New York. 1956

Steinbeck, John: **EAST OF EDEN.** Viking Press, New York. 1952

Wedertz, Frank S.: **BODIE: 1859-1900.** Sierra Media, Inc. Bishop, California. 1969

Whittaker, Peter: **THE AMERICAN WAY OF SEX.** Berkeley Publishing Corporation, New York. 1974

Waldorf, John Taylor: **A KID ON THE COMSTOCK.** American, West Publishing Co., Palo Alto, California. 1970

Walsh, Henry L.: **HALLOWED WERE THE GOLD DUST TRAITS,** University of Santa Clara Press. 1946

Order these Great books by mail today
by George Williams III

New! HOT SPRINGS OF THE EASTERN SIERRA Here are more than 40 natural hot spring pools author George Williams III has located from the Owens Valley, through the Eastern Sierra recreation corridor to Gerlach, Nevada. George has tracked down every hot spring worth "soaking" in. Included are many secret springs only known to locals. George gives easy to follow road directions and his "2 cents" about each spring are informative and entertaining. Maps by the author help you find these secret springs easily. 72 pages. AUTOGRAPHED. Soft cover, $6.95; hard cover, $12.95.

ROSA MAY: THE SEARCH FOR A MINING CAMP LEGEND Virginia City, Carson City and Bodie, California were towns Rosa May worked as a prostitute and madam 1873-1912. Read her remarkable true story based on 3 1/2 years of research. Praised by the Los Angeles Times and Las Vegas Review Journal. Includes 30 rare photos, 26 personal letters. 240 pages. AUTO-GRAPHED. Soft cover, $9.95; hard cover, $16.95. Soon to be a television movie.

THE REDLIGHT LADIES OF VIRGINIA CITY, NEVADA Virginia City was the richest mining camp in the American West. The silver from its mines built San Francisco and helped the Union win the Civil War. From 1860-95, Virginia City had one of the largest redlight districts in America. Here women from around the world worked the world's oldest profession. Author Williams tells the stories of the strange lives of the redlight girls, of their legends and violent deaths. Based on newspaper accounts, county records and U.S. Census information. Perhaps the best and most informative book on prostitution in the old West. Plenty of historic photos, illustrations and letters. 48 pages. AUTOGRAPHED. Soft cover, $5.95; hard cover, $10.95.

THE GUIDE TO BODIE AND EASTERN SIERRA HISTORIC SITES True story of the rise and fall of Bodie, California's most famous mining camp, today a ghost town, National Historic Site and California State Park. Known once as the toughest town in the West, murders were a daily occurrence in this mining town where millions were made in a few years. Has a beautiful full color cover with 100 photos on an 8 1/2 X 11 format. 88 pages. AUTOGRAPHED Soft cover, $9.95; hard cover, $16.95.

THE MURDERS AT CONVICT LAKE True story of the infamous 1871 Nevada State Penitentiary break in which 29 outlaws escaped and fled more than 250 miles into Mono and Inyo counties, California. They vowed to kill anyone who got in their way. In a terrible shootout at Monte Diablo, today known as Convict Lake just south of Mammoth lakes ski resort, the convicts killed two men. They fled to nearby Bishop where they were captured and hanged. Includes 18 rare photographs and pen and ink drawings by Dave Comstock, artist and author. 32 pages. AUTOGRAPHED. Soft cover, $4.95; hard cover, $9.95.

MARK TWAIN: HIS ADVENTURES AT AURORA AND MONO LAKE When Sam Clemens arrived in Nevada in 1861, he wanted to get rich quick. He tried silver mining at Aurora, Nevada near Mono Lake. Clemens didn't strike it rich but his hard luck mining days led to his literary career. Many rare photos and maps to places where Clemens lived, wrote and camped. 100 pages. AUTOGRAPHED. Soft cover, $6.95; hard cover, $12.95.

MARK TWAIN: HIS LIFE IN VIRGINIA CITY, NEVADA While reporting for the *Territorial Enterprise* in Virginia City, 1862-64, Sam Clemens adopted his now well known pen name, Mark Twain. Here is the lively account of Mark Twain's early writing days in the most exciting town in the West. Over 60 rare photos and maps to places Twain lived and wrote. 208 pages. AUTOGRAPHED. Soft cover, $9.95; hard cover, $24.95.

New for 1989! MARK TWAIN: JACKASS HILL AND THE JUMPING FROG In May, 1864, Mark Twain left Virginia City for San Francisco where he continued newspaper reporting for the San Francisco, *Morning Call*. Following trouble with the police, Twain retreated to Jackass Hill, near Sonora, in the Califonria Gold Rush country. Here during a three month stay he first heard the tale of "Jim Smiley and His Jumping Frog." Twain's version, published in November, 1865, made him an overnight celebrity. Here is the story of how it happened. 112 pages. Many rare photos and maps. AUTOGRAPHED. Soft cover, $6.95; hard cover, $12.95.

ORDER FORM

NAME_____ Address_____

City_____ State_____ ZIP_____

Please send me these books: _____

_____

_____

Total for books $_____

Add $1.50 postage first book. $.50 each additional book.

Total enclosed $_____

Mail to: **Tree By The River Publishing, PO Box 935 CL, Dayton, NV 89403**

Thanks for your mail order!!